MATH FAIR PROJECTS AND RESEARCH ACTIVITIES

A Comprehensive Guide for Students and Teachers

by Barry Doran
& Leland Graham

Incentive Publications, Inc.
Nashville, Tennessee

Acknowledgements
The authors would like to gratefully acknowledge the assistance and suggestions of the following people: Michelle Brouner, Sara Levy, Isabelle McCoy, Anne Poole, Stan Powell, Virginia Powell, and Connie York.

Illustrated by Marta Drayton
Cover by Marta Drayton
Edited by Patience Camplair

ISBN 0-86530-639-7

1 2 3 4 5 6 7 8 9 10   07   06   05   04

Table of Contents

INTRODUCTION

Math Fair Projects and Research Activities is organized as a resource for students and teachers who are looking for math fair project ideas. These math fair projects and research activities, which normally take three to eight weeks to complete, are a great way to provide students with some of their most valuable learning experiences based on different mathematical strands: number sense and operations; algebra, patterns, and relationships; geometry; measurement, time, and money; and data analysis and probability.

Some of the featured activities, such as note taking, making an outline, and creating a bibliography, have been designed so that they can be used by individuals or a group; however, some activities involve individual participation. Carefully read the instructions before beginning each chapter.

Since research is an integral part of the math project, students will be carefully guided through the step-by-step process of developing the thesis, introductory paragraph, body, and conclusion of their research paper. Included in this book is an example of a research paper for teachers to use as a guideline for students.

Also included in this book is a backboard section which is especially important for the actual math fair project. Even though a student's knowledge and understanding in writing the research paper may be excellent, if the backboard materials are not correctly displayed, the project will not receive its proper recognition. To further assist your students, we have included examples of various types of lettering, design elements, and examples of backboard sketches.

The Appendix contains a collection of helpful forms: Tips for Parents/Guardians, Sample Letters to Parents and Students, A Research Proposal Sheet, Suggested Project Rubric, Judge's Score Sheet, Math Resources, Checklist for the Completed Project, and a Reproducible Math Fair Certificate. Finally, we have included reproducible title cards which can be printed on card stock for use on the student's backboard.

Chapter One

MATHEMATICS STRANDS

Mathematics Strands

When beginning work on a mathematics project, it is important to focus on the various mathematics areas of study called strands. On the following pages, there are descriptions of each strand. Accompanying each strand are pictures, numbers, charts, graphs and figures that might inspire a topic choice. Chapter 14 has examples of backboard projects for each strand.

Number Sense and Operations

The number sense and operations strand is to mathematics what vocabulary is to language. Numbers are the "ABCs" of mathematics. Number sense includes recognizing different number names, counting, and arithmetic. Other examples include prime and composite, even and odd numbers, as well as square numbers, fractions, decimals, percents, and integers. Numbers have evolved from sanskrit to Roman numerals, and then to our present day base-ten number system. What would the number eight look like in sanskrit or Roman numerals?

Numbers allow us to compose other numbers by addition and multiplication, and to decompose numbers with subtraction and division. These are called number operations. How many ways are there to add, subtract, multiply, and divide? Can you find examples of different kinds of numbers around you?

Operations
+ − X ÷

Sanskrit 8
ᘹ
Roman Numeral 8
VIII

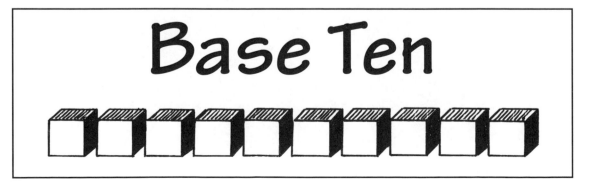

Base Ten

Algebra, Patterns, and Relationships

Algebra is the study of mathematical structure, number systems, and their properties. Problems are solved using arithmetic by substituting letters or symbols for numbers. As early as kindergarten, students solve problems like this: [ ] + 2 = 5. A place holder ([ ]) or a letter(a, x, y) in a number sentence or number expression (5y) is called a variable. By replacing a variable with different numbers, the result changes. Algebra studies how these changes affect number relationships.

Numerals

$2, \ .04, \ \frac{1}{3}, \ 10^2, \ -6$

Variables

a, x, y

Polynomials

$2x^2 + 3x + 7$

Expressions

$x + 2, \ y - 8$

Math Fair Projects and Research Activities

Geometry

Living in a 3-dimensional world requires that we recognize different geometric shapes such as prisms, cones, rectangular solids, and pyramids. Young children name and classify 2-dimensional shapes such as circles, squares, and triangles.

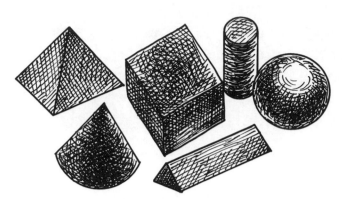

Geometric Solids

Refer to the diagram. For each pair given, write parallel, intersecting or perpendicular.

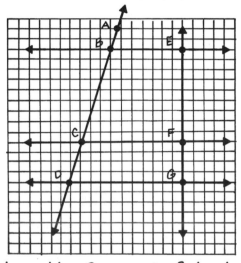

$\overleftrightarrow{AC}$ and $\overleftrightarrow{BE}$
Answer: intersecting

$\overleftrightarrow{EG}$ and $\overleftrightarrow{BE}$
Answer: perpendicular

$\overleftrightarrow{CD}$ and $\overleftrightarrow{CF}$
Answer: intersecting

$\overleftrightarrow{BE}$ and $\overleftrightarrow{CF}$
Answer: parallel

Lines, Line Segments & Angles

Geometry also includes the study of points, lines, line segments, angles, and coordinate planes. Other geometry topics include slides, flips, turns, symmetry and congruence, geometric construction, and topology.

Architects use geometry to design buildings, and engineers use geometry to build roads and bridges. Artists use geometry to paint pictures. Is there geometry in music? The food that we buy at the grocery store comes packaged in geometric shapes like boxes, cans, and bottles. Can you find examples of geometry in your house?

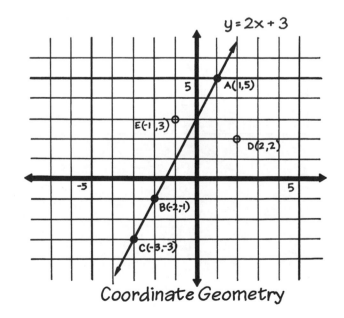

Coordinate Geometry

Math Fair Projects and Research Activities

Measurement, Time, and Money

Measurement, time, and money are the most widely used applications of mathematics. "How much taller am I than my sister?" "How much does my dog weigh?" "How far is it to the mall?" "What time do the cartoons come on TV?" "How much does a new bicycle cost?" All of these are examples of how we use measurement every day. Measurement tools include rulers, yard sticks, meter sticks, containers such as cups, pints, quarts, gallons and liters, scales, and clocks.

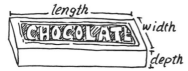

There are two systems of measurement—the U.S. customary or English system that includes inches, feet, yards, ounces, pounds, cups, and pints, and the metric system that includes millimeters, centimeters, meters, liters, and grams.

Which measurement system does most of the world use? How does the U.S. customary system compare to the metric system?

Math Fair Projects and Research Activities

Data Analysis and Probability

Information is all around us in books, newspapers, and the World Wide Web. Data analysis allows us to collect, organize, and display large amounts of data so that we can learn from it. Data can be displayed in charts, graphs, or tables. Some of the most common graphs are pictographs, pie graphs, bar graphs, and line graphs. What other types of graphs can you find? Determining the range, mean, median, and mode of a set of numbers can also be used to organize and interpret data. How do you find the batting average for your favorite baseball player?

Probability is the area of mathematics that explores the likelihood or chance that a certain event will or will not occur. "What is the chance of rain tomorrow?" "If I roll a pair of dice, what is the chance or probability of rolling two sixes?" You can use experiments to predict and test probability. For example, if you flip a penny 100 times, predict how many heads and how many tails will result. Flip a penny 100 times and record the number of heads and tails. How close was your prediction to the results of your experiment? The results of your experiment can be displayed in a chart, table, or graph.

Math Fair Projects and Research Activities

Chapter Two

SELECTING A MATHEMATICS TOPIC

Selecting a Mathematics Topic

The most important step in creating a mathematics project is choosing a topic. In selecting a topic, refer to the five mathematics strands described in Chapter One. Use the guidelines listed below in choosing a topic.

1. Avoid a topic that is too broad.

    EXAMPLE: **What is geometry?**

    It is impossible to include all the information that would be needed to answer this broad question.

    BETTER TOPIC: **What are the platonic solids and why are there five?**

2. Avoid a topic that is too limited.

    EXAMPLE: **What are even and odd numbers?**

    If a question can be answered in a few words or sentences, it is too limited.

    BETTER TOPIC: **Why does 2n always produce an even number and 2n+1 always produce an odd number?**

3. Avoid a topic that could be dangerous to you, or that may be illegal.

    Such a project probably will not be admitted to a local fair.

4. Avoid a topic about which people throughout the world cannot agree.

    EXAMPLE: **Why do some people not like math?**

    BETTER TOPIC: **How does math anxiety affect student performance?**

5. Avoid a topic which is confusing because it is not clear what information is requested.

    EXAMPLE: **Can a computer do math?**

    BETTER TOPIC: **How does a computer add?**

What Makes a Successful Mathematics Project?

A mathematics fair project offers you the opportunity to research and learn about things that interest you. Mathematics fair projects teach you problem-solving skills, help to improve your oral and written communication skills, and provide you with self-satisfaction for producing a well-done project. A mathematics project is more than just a research paper, a visual display of data, or a mathematical model. It allows you to demonstrate a thorough understanding of your selected topic of study. Use the guidelines below to begin designing a good project.

1. **Select a topic in which you are interested.**
   The key to a successful mathematics project is selecting a topic that interests you. You will do a better job on your project if it is a topic that motivates you. It can even be fun!

2. **Decide what type of investigation fits your topic.**
   After choosing a topic, decide how to conduct your experiment or research. You can perform an investigation if you want to find out how manipulating different variables can change the outcome. You can also choose to conduct surveys (for almost any topic). Surveys provide data that can be organized, analyzed, and displayed in tables, charts, or graphs to answer your research question. You may decide to build models to help you understand how something works. For example, what geometric design makes the strongest bridge?

3. **Do your own work.**
   Make sure your mathematics fair project is your own work. As a student you may receive assistance in choosing your topic and designing your project, but the final effort must be yours. Use your own creativity and ingenuity to conduct your investigation and you will gain a better understanding of why things do or do not work as you had hoped.

4. **Know your research well.**
   You need to investigate your topic as completely as possible. Can you explain your investigation and your results in your own words to your teacher or a friend? Can you think of other questions related to your topic? Can you explain your results in a written summary and with photographs, charts, graphs, diagrams, tables, or drawings? If so, you probably have a great mathematics project!

Math Fair Projects and Research Activities

Can You Write a Good Topic Question?

A good mathematics topic is one which enables you to use everyday experiences to compare, investigate, or model the question. Read the real-world situations below and write a possible topic question.

1. Lee Nakato goes to a Japanese school where he studies mathematics using the Kumon Method. Lennie Mitchell, his neighbor and best friend, goes to the middle school down the street and studies mathematics the "traditional" way.

   Topic Question: _____

   _____

   _____

2. In August, compare the mean, median, and range of heights for males and females in your class at school. Measure again in January.

   Topic Question: _____

   _____

   _____

3. The game "Rock, Paper, Scissors" has three moves. Use statistics to show how many times "scissors" comes up.

   Topic Question: _____

   _____

   _____

4. In an experiment, Andy flips a coin 10 times and gets "heads" 7 times. He knows that the hypothetical odds should be 5 "heads" in 10 flips.

Topic Question: _____

_____

_____

5. Kimberly reaches into a bag of colored candies and gets a red one. The next time she also gets a red one.

Topic Question: _____

_____

_____

17

Choosing a Topic

(To the Teacher)

Objectives:

1. The students will select a topic and write an appropriate question for their mathematics project.

2. The students will conduct a mathematics search to determine the availability of materials.

Procedures:

1. In class, have a brainstorming session to list topics of current interest.

   a. Eliminate irrelevant mathematics topics.

   b. Eliminate topics that are too broad or too limited.

   c. Eliminate topics that are not original.

2. Have students continue brainstorming at home in order to select a topic of interest to them.

3. Have students complete Section I of the Research Proposal Sheet (page 109)

4. Have students go to the library and search for information that answers the proposed question. Have students list the available sources on the back of the proposal sheet. Do not forget to suggest periodicals, almanacs, government publications, encyclopedias, letters, biographical dictionaries, and books on the subject. List ideas for conducting surveys, interviews, and observations. Decide on other useful mathematics methods for gathering information, such as visiting areas of significance, taking photos, or writing letters.

5. Have students complete Section II of the proposal sheet (see page 109).

6. After approval, have students complete Section III of the proposal sheet (see page 109) to outline strategies for answering their questions.

7. Ask students to have a parent or guardian sign the proposal sheet.

Evaluation:

The students will successfully write a research question and an outline of strategies that meets the teacher's approval.

Chapter Three

SUGGESTED MATHEMATICS TOPIC INVESTIGATIONS

Suggested Mathematics Topic Investigations

Traditionally, there have not been many mathematics projects in science fairs. One explanation for this might be that it is not clear what a mathematics project involves. The following list of possible project investigations could make exciting and interesting mathematics fair projects. You may find some are more interesting to you than others, while some may require more of a mathematics background than others.

Most mathematics fairs are separated into two categories: Junior Division (grades 5–8) and Senior Division (grades 9–12). The suggested investigations that follow have been divided into these two divisions, followed by some general mathematics topics and a list of mathematicians that could be researched to investigate what contributions each has made to the field of mathematics.

Junior Division Suggested Investigations

Number Sense:

- Investigate "big" numbers. What is a big number? A bank is robbed of 1 million dollars. How long would it take to move that much money? How much would it weigh? How much space would it fill? What is the biggest number that has ever been written? What does this number represent?

- Study the golden mean. It appears in art, architecture, biology, and geometry, and is connected to the Fibonacci Numbers. What is the golden mean and where does it appear?

- Find out all you can about the Fibonacci Numbers: 0, 1, 2, 3, 5, 8 . . . Where do they appear in nature?

- Find out all you can about the Catalan Numbers: 1, 2, 5, 14, 42 . . .

- Investigate the creation of secret codes (ciphers). Find out where they are used today and how they have been used throughout history. Build your own cipher using prime numbers.

- What are Napier's Bones and what can you do with them?

- How do computer bar codes work? What is coding theory and how does it work?

- Look at number systems based on numbers other than 10. How are they used in other cultures?

- Explore the history and use of the Abacus. Make a model.

- Infinity comes in different "sizes." How can this be explained? Investigate number theory.

- There are several methods of counting and calculating using your fingers and hands. Explore the mathematics behind each method.

Geometry and Measurement:

- Investigate the regular solids (platonic and Archimedean), their properties, geometry, and occurrence in nature. Build models.

- Build rigid and non-rigid geometric structures. Explore them. Where are rigid structures used? Find unusual applications.

- Investigate the history of pi and the many ways in which it can be approximated. Calculate new digits of pi.

- Consider tiling a plane using shapes of the same size (i.e., any 4-sided shape). What is possible and what is not? What about 5-sided shapes?

- There is a traditional Chinese method of illustrating the Pythagorean Theorem using paper. Investigate and make models.

Probability and Statistics:

- Compare the mean, median, and range of heights for male and female students in your class. How will they compare to a class one year older?

- What is the probability of picking a red candy out of a bag?

- How can you use the game of "Rock, Paper, Scissors" to demonstrate statistics?

- What is the fewest number of colors needed to color any map if no two countries with a common border can have the same color? Who discovered this proof?

General Topic Investigations:

- Investigate knots. What happens when you put a knot in a strip of paper and flatten it carefully? When is what appears to be a knot really a knot? Look for methods for drawing knots.

- What is game theory all about and where is it applied?

- Investigate the history and mathematics of symmetry. Construct a kaleidoscope to demonstrate your research.

- Investigate card tricks and magic tricks based in mathematics. Some of the best in the world were designed by mathematician/statistician Persi Diaconis.

Math Fair Projects and Research Activities

Senior Division Suggested Investigations

Number Sense:

- Investigate triangular numbers. Also research square, pentagonal, and hexagonal numbers. Are there numbers in the third and fourth dimensions?

- Is there an algorithm for getting out of two-dimensional mazes? What about three-dimensional? Investigate the history of mazes.

- Explore Egyptian fractions.

- Build models to illustrate asymptotic results such as the prime number theorem.

- There is a device for illustrating the binomial distribution. Marbles are dropped through the top and encounter a series of pins before dropping into cells where they are distributed according to the binomial distribution. How would changing the position of the pins affect the kinds of distributions (bimodal, skewed, rectangular, etc.)? Explore.

Algebra, Calculus, and Discrete Mathematics:

- At certain times during the week, trash is collected in your neighborhood. It is often collected in a particular geographical area at one time. The problem, once pick up location is determined, is to decide on the most efficient routes to make the collections. Find out how this is done and investigate improving the procedure. Hint: Research graph theory.

- How are fire stations located in order to best serve the needs of the community? Hint: graph theory again!

- How does the NBA work out the basketball schedule? How would you complete such a schedule, keeping in mind distances between game locations, home team advantage, etc.? Could you devise a good schedule for one of your local teams?

- How do major hospitals schedule the use of operating theatres? Are they allowing the maximum number of operations to be done each day?

Geometry and Measurement:

- Build a physical model based on dissections to prove the Pythagorean Theorem.

- Investigate the cycloid curve. Include its properties and its history.

- Discover all seventeen "different" kinds of wallpaper. How is this related to the work of M. C. Escher? Discover the history of this problem. Hint: Research triangulated patterns and frieze patterns.

- Draw and list any interesting properties of various curves such as evolutes, involutes, roulettes, pedal curves, conchoids, cissoids, strophoids, caustics, spirals, and ovals.

- Find as many triangles as you can with integer sides and a simple linear relation between the angles. What happens when the triangle is a right triangle?

- What is Morley's triangle? Can you draw a picture of the 18 Morley triangles associated with a given triangle ABC?

- What is a hexaflexagon? Make as many different ones as you can.

- Build models showing that parallelograms with the same base and height have the same area. This can lead to a purely visual proof of the Pythagorean Theorem.

- What is fractal dimension? Investigate it by studying examples that show what happens to lines, areas, solids, and the Koch curve when you double the scale.

- The Parabolic Reflector Microphone is used at sporting events to hear one person in a noisy area. Investigate and explain the mathematics behind what is happening.

General Topic Investigations:

- Investigate the Steiner problem—one application of which concerns the location of telephone exchanges.

- Construct a double pendulum and use it to investigate chaos.

- What are Pick's Theorem and Euler's Theorem? Investigate them separately, or try to discover how they are related.

- Use proportional-integral-differential (PID) controllers and oscilloscopes to demonstrate the integration and differentiation of various functions.

- Learn about origamic architecture by making pop-up greeting cards.

- Discover how to construct the Koch or "snowflake" curve. Use a computer to draw fractals based on simple equations such as Julia sets and Mandelbrot sets.

Source: Math Projects for Science Fairs. Canadian Mathematical Society. http://www.cms.math.ca/Education/mpsf/

Math Fair Projects and Research Activities

Mathematicians Through the Ages

Researching the lives and the accomplishments of famous mathematicians makes an excellent project for both the Junior and Senior Divisions of a mathematics fair. For a comprehensive list of mathematicians, visit http://aleph0.clarku.edu/~djoyce/mathhist/chronology.html

A

Abel, Niels, 1802–1829
Ahmes or Ahmose, 1500 B.C.
Aiken, Howard, 1900–
Al Khowarizmi, 9th Century A.D.
Anaxagoras, 500?–428 B.C.
Apollonius, 260–200 B.C.
Archimedes of Samos, 287–212 B.C.
Aristotle, 384–322 B.C.
Atwood, George, 1746–1807

B

Babbage, Charles, 1792–1871
Bacon, Roger, 1214–1294
Beltrami, Eugenio, 1835–1900
Bernoulli Family, 1654–1782
Bhaskara, Boethius, 475–525
Bolyai, Johann, 1802–1860
Boole, George, 1815–1865
Brahe, Tycho, 1546–1601
Briggs, Henry, 1561–1630
Brouwer, Luityen, 1881–1950
Bush, Vannevar, 1890–1966

C

Cantor, Georg, 1845–1918
Cardano, Girolamo, 1501–1576
Carroll, Lewis, 1832–1898
Cauchy, Augustin Louis, 1789–1857
Cavalieri, Francesco, 1598–1647
Cayley, Arthur, 1821–1895
Copernicus, Nicholas, 1473–1543

D

D'Alembert, Jean, 1717–1783
Dedekind, Richard, 1831–1916

DeMere, Antoine Lombard, 1610–1684
Democritus, 460–370 B.C.
DeMoivre, Abraham, 1667–1754
DeMorgan, Augustus, 1806–1871
Desargues, Gerard, 1593–1662
Descartes, Rene, 1596–1650
Diophantus, ?–320 A.D.
Durer, Albrecht, 1471–1528

E

Einstein, Albert, 1879–1955
Eratosthenes, 275–195 B.C.
Euclid, about 300 B.C.
Eudoxus, 408–355 B.C.
Euler, Leonhard, 1707–1783

F

Fermat, Pierre de, 1601–1665
Ferro, Scipio, 1462–1526
Frege, Gottlob, 1848–1925

G

Galilei, Galileo, 1564–1642
Galois, Evariste, 1811–1832
Galton, Sir Francis, 1822–1911
Gauss, Karl Friedrich, 1777–1855
Girard, Albert, 1595–1632
Gunter, Edmund, 1581–1626

H

Hamilton, Sir William, 1805–1865
Harriot, Thomas, 1560–1621
Hermite, Charles, 1822–1901
Hero of Alexandria, (Heron), 2nd Century B.C.
Hilbert, David, 1862–1943
Hipparchus, 2nd Century B.C.
Hippocrates, 440? B.C.

J

Jacobi, Carl, 1804–1851
Jones, William, 1675–1749

K

Kasner, Edward, 1878–1955
Kelvin, Lord, 1824–1907
Kepler, Johannes, 1571–1630
Klein, Felix, 1849–1925

L

Lagrange, Joseph Louis, 1736–1813
Laplace, Pierre Simon de, 1749–1827
Legendre, Adrien-Marie, 1752–1833
Leibnitz, Baron Gottfried Wilhelm, 1646–1716
Leonardo of Pisa, 1175–1230
Lobachevski, Nikolai, 1793–1856
Ludolph, van Ceulen, 17th Century A.D.

M

Maclaurin, Colin, 1698–1746
Maxwell, James Clerk, 1831–1879
Menaechmus, 375–325 B.C.
Mendel, Gregor, 1833–1884
Menelaus A.D. 100
Mobius, August Ferdinand, 1790–1868
Montessori, Maria, 1870–1952

N

Napier, John, 1550–1617
Newton, Sir Isaac, 1642–1727
Nichomachus, 1st Century A.D.

O

Omar Khayyam, A.D. 1100
Oresme, Nicole, 1323–1382
Oughtred, William, 1575–1660

P

Pappus, A.D. 300
Pascal, Blaise, 1623–1662
Peano, Giuseppe, 1858–1932
Plato, 429–347 B.C.
Poincare, Jules Henri, 1854–1912
Polya, George, 1887–1985
Poncelet, Jean Victor, 1788–1867
Ptolemy, 100–168
Pythagoras, 582–507 B.C.

Q

Quetelet, Lambert Adolphe, 1796–1874

R

Rademacher, Hans, 1892–1969
Rado, Tibor, 1895–1965
Ramanujan, Srinivasa, 1887–1920
Razmadze, Andrei, 1889–1929
Riemann, Georg, 1826–1866
Riesz, Marcel, 1886–1969
Ritt, Joseph, 1893–1951
Russell, Sir Bertrand, 1872–1970

S

Schmidt, Erhard, 1876–1959
Schrodinger, Erwin, 1887–1961
Schur, Issai, 1875–1941
Severi, Francesco, 1879–1961
Sheffer, Henry, 1883–1964
Sierpinski, Waclaw, 1882–1969
Skolem, Albert Thoralf, 1887–1963
Steinhaus, Hugo Dyonizy, 1887–1972
Steinitz, Ernst, 1871–1928
Steffensen, Johan Frederik, 1873–1961
Stoilow, Simion, 1887–1961
Szasz, Otto, 1884–1952

T

Takagi, Teiji, 1875–1960
Tartaglia, Niccolo, 1499–1557
Thales, 640–546 B.C.
Thebault, Victor, 1882–1960
Tietze, Heinrich, 1880–1964
Toeplitz, Otto, 1881–1940
Tzitzeica, Gheorghe, 1873–1939

U

Uccello, Paolo, 1397–1475

V

Venn, John, 1834–1923
Vieta, Francois, 1540–1603

W

Weierstrass, Karl, 1815–1897
Whitehead, Alfred North, 1861–1947

Mathematicians Through the Ages
How Good Are Your Research Skills?

Directions: Use an encyclopedia or the Internet to match these famous mathematicians with their major accomplishments.

____ 1. Baron Gottfried Wilhelm Von Leibniz

____ 2. Jean Victor Poncelet

____ 3. Aristotle

____ 4. Pythagoras

____ 5. Pierre Simon de Laplace

____ 6. George Boole

____ 7. John Napier

____ 8. Karl Weierstrass

____ 9. Ptolemy

____ 10. Charles Babbage

a. His mathematics work influenced the production of atomic energy. (1815–1897)

b. He is best remembered for his theory on the continuity of numbers. (1788–1867)

c. He is best know for his geometric theorem of a right triangle. (588–507 B.C.)

d. He was the first to give pi an estimated value of 3.1416. (100–146)

e. He is credited with inventing Calculus, the chief advancement in mathematics during the first half of the 18th Century. (1646–1716)

f. A French mathematician who, with Bernoulli, was one of the originators of the field of probability. (1749–1867)

g. A great Greek philosopher who laid the foundation for most of the branches of science and philosophy known today. (384–322 B.C.)

h. An English mathematician who helped develop modern symbolic logic. (1815–1865)

i. He invented a calculating machine that was the forerunner of today's computers. (1792–1871)

j. He invented a multiplication device for improving the Abacus which was the forerunner of the slide rule. (1550–1617)

Name _____

Mathematicians Through the Ages

Timeline of Mathematicians

Directions: Place the mathematicians listed below on the timeline showing when they were born.

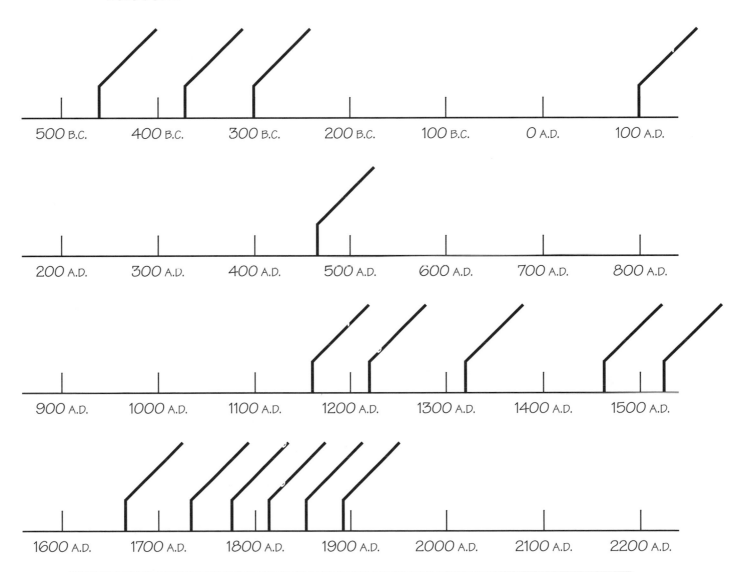

Aristotle 384 B.C.

Charles Babbage 1792 A.D.

Roger Bacon 1214 A.D.

Boethius Bhaskara 475 A.D.

George Boole 1815 A.D.

Nicholas Copernicus 1473 A.D.

Democritus 460 B.C.

Vannevar Bush 1890 A.D.

Albert Einstein 1879 A.D..

Euclid 300 B.C.

Galileo Galilei 1564 A.D.

Karl Friedrich Gauss 1777 A.D.

William Jones 1675 A.D.

Leonardo of Pisa 1175 A.D.

Nicole Oresme 1323 A.D.

Ptolemy 100 A.D.

Math Fair Projects and Research Activities

Famous Women Mathematicians

Over the last five centuries, women have contributed to the advancements of mathematics. Listed below is an alphabetical index of famous women mathematicians.

A

Maria Gaetana Agnesi, 1718–1799
Florence Eliza Allen, 1876–?
Annie Dale Biddle Andrews 1885–1940
Hertha Ayrton, 1854–1923

B

Grace M. Bareis, 1875–1962
Nina Karlovna Bari, 1901–1962
Ruth Aaronsom Bari, 1917–?
Charlotte Barnum, 1860–1934
Agnes Baxter, 1870–1917
Alexandra Bellow, 1935–
Dorothy Lewis Bernstein, 1914–1988
Joan S. Birman, 1927–
Gerthrude Blanch, 1898–1996
Lenore Blum, 1943–
Mary Everest Boole, 1832–1916
Marjorie Lee Browne, 1914–1979
Josephine E. Burns, 1887–?

C

Mary Lucy Cartwright, 1900–1998
Sun-Yung Alice Chang, 1948–
Emilie du Chatelet, 1706–1749
Yvonne Choquet-Bruhat, 1923–
Fan Chung, 1949–
Maria Cinquini-Cibrario, 1905–1992
Gertrude Mary Cox, 1900–1978
Louise Duffield Cummings, 1870–1947
Susan Jane Cunningham, 1842–1921

D

Ingrid Daubechies, 1954–
Florence Nightingale David, 1909–1993
Elizabeth Dickerson, 1872–1954

F

Etta Falconer, 1933–2002
Sister Mary Celine Fasenmyer, 1906–1996
Kate Fenchel, 1905–1983
Annie MacKinnon Fitch, 1868–1940
Irmgard Flugge-Lotz, 1903–1974

G

Hilda Geiringer von Mises, 1893–1973
Ruth Gentry, 1862–1917
Sophie Germain, 1776–1831
Evelyn Boyd Granville, 1924–
Mary Gray, 1938–

H

Margaret Jarman Hagood, 1908–1963
Louise Hay, 1935–1989
Ellen Amanda Hayes, 1851–1930
Euphemia Lofton Haynes, 1890–1980
Nola Haynes, 1897–1996
Olive Clio Hazlett, 1890–1974
Cora Barbara Hennel, 1886–1947
Caroline Herschel, 1750–1848
Hu Hesheng, 1928–
Gloria Hewitt, 1935–
Grace Brewster Murray Hopper, 1906–1992
Hypatia, 370?–415

Math Fair Projects and Research Activities   Copyright ©2004 by Incentive Publications, Inc., Nashville, TN.

J

Sofja Aleksandrovna Janovskaja, 1896–1966

K

Carol Karp, 1926–1972

Linda Keen, 1940–

Claribel Kendall, 1889–1965

Ada Byron King, Countess of Lovelace,
    1815–1852

Nancy Kopell, 1942–

Sofia Kovalevskaya, 1850–1891

Cecilia Krieger, 1894–1974

Krystyna Kuperberg, 1944

L

Christine Ladd-Franklin, 1847–1930

Olga Alexandrovna Ladyzhenskaya, 1922–

Edna Kramer Lassar, 1902–1984

Marguerite Lehr, 1898–1988

Elizaveta Fedorovna Litvinova, 1845–1919

Marie Litzinger, 1899–1952

Mayme I. Logsdon, 1881–1967

M

Sheila Scott Macintyre, 1910–1960

F. Jessie MacWilliams, 1917–1990

Isabel Maddison, 1869–1950

Vivienne Malone-Mayes, 1932–1995

Emilie Norton Martin, 1869–1936

Vera Nikoaevna Maslennikova, 1926–

Dorothy McCoy, 1903–2001

Dusa McDuff, 1945–

Helen Abbot Merrill, 1864–1949

Winifred Edgerton Merrill, 1862–1951

Ida Metcalf, 1857–1952

Cathleen Morawetz, 1923–

Ruth Moufang, 1905–1977

N

Evelyn M. Nelson, 1943–1987

Hanna Neumann, 1914–1971

Mary Frances Winston Newson, 1869–1959

Florence Nightingale, 1820–1910

Emmy Noether, 1882–1935

O

Olga Arsen'enva Oleinik, 1925–2001

Helen Brewster Owens, 1881–1968

P

Leona May Peirce, 1863–1954

Charlotte Elvira Pengra, 1875–1916

Bernadette Perrin-Riou, 1955–

Rozsa Peter, 1905–1977

Sophie Piccard, 1904–

Elena Lucrezia Cornaro Piscopia, 1646–1684

Vera Pless, 1931–

Pelageya Yakovlevna Polubarinova-Kochina,
    1899–

Cheryl Praeger, 1948–

R

Virginia Ragsdale, 1870–1945

Marina Ratner, 1938–

Nancy Reid, 1952–

Mina Rees, 1902–1997

Julia Bowman Robinson, 1919–1985

Mary Ross, 1908–

Linda Rothschild, 1945–

Mary Ellen Rudin, 1924–

S

Cora Ratto de Sadosky, 1912–1981

Judith D. Sally, 1937–

Jane Cronin Scanlon, 1922–

Alice T. Schafer, 1915–
Doris Schattschneider, 1939–
Lesley Sibner, 1934–
Lao Genevra Simons, 1870–1949
Mary Emily Sinclair, 1878–1955
Clara Eliza Smith, 1865–1943
Karen E. Smith, 1965–
Pauline Sperry, 1885–1967
Bhama Srinivasan, 1935–
Alicia Boole Stott, 1860–1940
Lorna Mary Swain, 1891–1936

T

Olga Taussky-Todd, 1906–1995
Jean Taylor, 1944–
Bird Margaret Turner, 1877–1962

U

Karen Uhlenbeck, 1942–

V

Argelia Velez-Rodriguez, 1936–
Roxana Hayward Vivian,1871–?

W

Mary Catherine Bishop Weiss, 1930–1966
Anna Pell Wheeler, 1931–
Mary F. Wheeler, 1931–
Ruth Goulding Wood, 1875–

Y

Anna Irwin Young, 1873–1920
Grace Chisholm Young, 1868–1944
Lai-Sang Young, 1952–

Winifred Edgerton Merrill

1862–1951

The First American Woman
to Receive a Ph.D. in Mathematics

For a more complete list, visit Biographies of Women Mathematicians at
http://www.agnesscott.edu/lriddle/women/women.htm

Famous Women Mathematicians

Directions: Choose a famous woman mathematician from the alphabetical list on the previous pages. Research the contributions she made to mathematics. Record your facts on the graphic organizer below.

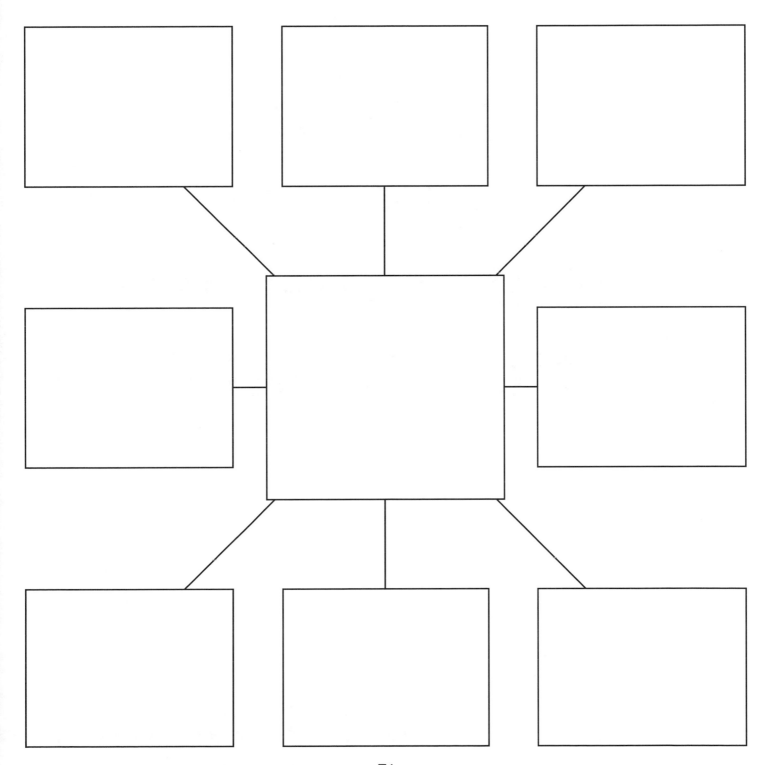

Math Fair Projects and Research Activities

Chapter Four

SUGGESTED MATH FAIR PROJECT TIMELINE AND DUE DATES

Suggested Math Fair
Project Timeline and Due Dates

(To the teacher)

Teachers can help students organize their math fair project by breaking the tasks into manageable chunks and assigning specific due dates for different parts. Provide students with a timeline of due dates for their question, experimental design, draft reports, results, display layout design, and final report. You may want to give students a chance to work on portions of their project in class. Working with other students during math and language arts classes, as well as library/media center time, can be a valuable way for students to obtain and share ideas for improving their projects. This time also gives you a chance to clarify your expectations for their projects.

The following suggested timeline and due dates may be helpful in planning a successful math fair project.

Student Timeline and Due Dates

Week 1   Choose a Math Topic   Date _____

_____ Choose a topic and have it approved by your teacher.

_____ Start a list of possible resources.

_____ Begin reading materials appropriate to your topic.

_____ Establish a project journal or logbook.

Week 2   Refine Your Topic Question   Date _____

_____ Form a hypothesis and state what you plan to prove or explain.

_____ Write, call, or email outside sources such as businesses, universities, and governmental agencies for additional information.

_____ Begin a research plan, including your question or problem, hypothesis, procedures, and bibliography.

_____ Submit your research plan to your teacher for approval.

Math Fair Projects and Research Activities

Week 3 Collect Materials/Equipment for Your Investigation   Date _____

_____ Set up your investigation/experiment.

_____ Learn how to use any needed equipment. Ask adults for help, if necessary.

_____ Record procedures in your journal or logbook.

Week 4 Collect Data   Date _____

_____ Begin testing, experimenting, or constructing your investigation.

_____ Adjust your research plans as data is collected from your testing.

_____ Record notes and observations in your journal or logbook.

_____ Take photographs of your research project in progress.

_____ Read collected information for background about your topic and record notes in your journal or logbook.

_____ Become an expert on your topic.

Week 5 Write Note Cards and Continue Research   Date _____

_____ Use what you have learned to begin writing note cards.

_____ Continue experimentation.

_____ Consult experts regarding your experimental design.

_____ Review books, articles, and Internet resources for additional information.

_____ Continue recording notes, making observations, and collecting information for your note cards.

_____ Consult with your teacher.

Week 6 Begin Rough Draft   Date _____

_____ Begin preparing titles, labels, graphs, drawings, and photographs for your display.

_____ Start the analysis of data collected.

_____ Begin writing a first draft of your research paper including a statement of your problem, hypothesis, preliminary information, and bibliography.

_____ Submit your rough draft to your teacher.

Week 7   Write Second Draft   Date _____

_____ Use your teacher's comments to correct any mistakes in your first draft.

_____ Review analysis of data and results. Make note cards for each.

_____ Write second draft of your research paper to include analysis of data, evaluation of possible solutions, and conclusion. The conclusion should restate your purpose, include the findings of your research, and state conclusions based on your data.

Week 8   Construct Display Board   Date _____

_____ Begin designing and constructing your display board.

_____ Write the text of your background information for your display board.

_____ Complete charts, graphs, drawings, and computer-generated visual aids for your display board.

_____ Continue work on the draft of your research paper.

Week 9   Complete Final Draft and Display Board   Date _____

_____ Type your final research paper. Your paper should be approximately 600 words or less.

_____ Finalize background text by using concise wording and bullets. Mount on your display board.

_____ Carefully check your display for spelling, punctuation, and grammar.

_____ Mount graphs, charts, drawings, and photographs on your display board.

_____ Check rules governing display materials and other allowable items.

Week 10 Conduct a Final Check   Date _____

_____ Proofread your typed research paper. It should be completely free of errors.

_____ Set up your display at home in order to check for flaws or mistakes.

_____ Practice presenting your research and answering potential questions about your project that the judges may ask you.

_____ Make sure all required forms are completed. Do not forget to include your journal or logbook, research paper (including bibliography), and any other items needed to complete your display.

Math Fair Projects and Research Activities

Chapter Five

FORMAT AND STEPS FOR THE RESEARCH PAPER

Format and Steps for the Research Paper

A paper describing your research is required and should be displayed in your research project notebook, along with any necessary forms or other relevant materials. Before you begin, check for any special rules that your teacher may require. A good research paper includes the following sections:

1. **Title Page**—This page includes the project title, student's name, address, school, and grade.

2. **Table of Contents**—As you finish writing, number each section.

3. **Introduction**—The introduction should explain the background information about your topic and the reason behind your choice of study. Refer to previous research as well as your own experiment(s). Establish a strong rationale for the study by emphasizing unresolved issues or questions. Conclude by stating the research hypothesis.

4. **Materials and Procedure** (if required)—Describe in detail the methods used to derive your data and your observations. Use photographs and drawings of your equipment to further describe your experiment(s). Include a precise description of the sample, any apparatus that was constructed or modified for the study, and methods of data collection.

5. **Results**—Present the data collected in the experiment(s) in tables and graphs; summarize the data in narrative form. Include statistical analysis of the data. Do not include raw data. Use only information collected during the current year's study.

6. **Discussion**—Your results and conclusions should flow smoothly and logically from your data. Be thorough. Compare your results with theoretical values, published data, commonly held beliefs, and/or expected results. A complete paper should include a discussion of possible errors or problems experienced.

7. **Conclusion**—Briefly summarize your results. Discuss whether or not your data supported your hypothesis and what your next steps in experimentation may be.

8. **Acknowledgements/Credits**—Credit assistance received from mentors, parents, teachers, and other sources.

9. **References/Bibliography**—Your reference list should include any material that is not your own (i.e., books, websites, papers, journal articles, and communications cited in the paper). Follow the samples shown in the bibliography section of this book (pages 41-44).

10. **Appendix**—Include critical information that is too lengthy for the main section of the paper, such as raw data, additional tables and graphs, copies of surveys and tests, and diagrams of equipment.

Math Fair Projects and Research Activities

Chapter Six

USING THE SCIENTIFIC METHOD

The Scientific Method

The scientific method is a step-by-step procedure which is used to determine the answer to any scientific question. Therefore, it is an essential part of conductiing the research and experimentation for your mathematics fair project paper. Below are the six steps in the scientific method.

1. PROBLEM: .... Identify a problem or question to investigate.

2. HYPOTHESIS: .... State what you think the result of your investigation will be.

3. MATERIALS: .... State the materials that you will use in your experiment.

4. PROCEDURE: .... Complete a step-by-step explanation of your experiment. Follow the steps to test your hypothesis.

5. RESULTS: .... Make observations and take notes about what you observed.

6. CONCLUSION: .... Reach your conclusion after observing the data.

The Importance of The Scientific Method

The scientific method will allow you to use a sensible problem-solving approach to answer your question. If you encounter a problem, or if your experiment should fail, then the scientific method will provide remedies to make logical changes in your experiment. It also allows you as a scientist to repeat or copy another scientist's experiment. If the experiment cannot be copied, then the conclusions derived from the original experiment may be questioned. In this way, the scientific method allows for experiments, results, and conclusions to be duplicated.

Math Fair Projects and Research Activities

Chapter Seven

BIBLIOGRAPHY CARDS AND NOTE TAKING

Bibliography Cards

If a student plans to use information from a particular source (book, encyclopedia, magazine, Internet, interview, survey, or pamphlet), he or she must record and keep certain information for the bibliography. The information can be recorded on 3" x 5" index cards, which will make it easier to create a bibliography.

When writing bibliography cards, write a number in the upper right-hand corner of each note card for easy organization and reference. Depending on the type of resource used, different information will need to be recorded on the bibliography card.

Record the following information for a book:
1. Name of the author (last name first)
2. Title of the book (underlined)
3. Place of publication (city)
4. Name of the publisher
5. Year of publication (most recent year)

```
                                                    4

    Hightower, Paul. Galileo Astronomer

    and Physicist. Berkeley Heights:

    Enslow Publishers, Inc., 1997.
```

Note: *A comma is placed between the author's last and first names. A period is placed after the author's name and book title. A colon is placed after the city, and a comma is inserted between the publisher and the year. A period is placed after the year.*

Math Fair Projects and Research Activities

Record the following information for an encyclopedia:

1. Name of the author of the article (if an author is listed)
2. Title of the article (in quotation marks)
3. Title of the encyclopedia (underlined)
4. Year of publication (edition)

1

Bunch, Bryan H. "Mathematics."
The New Book of Knowledge. 1983.

Note: If the article has an author, a comma is placed between the author's last and first names. A period is placed after the entire name. A period is placed at the end of article title and before the closing quotation marks. A period is also placed after the name of the encyclopedia.

2

"Fibonacci Numbers." World Book
Encyclopedia. 2000.

Record the following information for a magazine or newspaper:

1. Name of the author (if one is given)
2. Title of the article (in quotation marks)
3. Name of the magazine or newspaper (underlined)
4. Date of the magazine or newspaper
5. Page number(s) of the article

```
                                              5

   "Leonardo DaVinci." Math History.

   March, 1999: 20–23.

```

Note: *A comma is placed between the author's last and first names. A period is placed after the entire name. A comma is placed between the month and year. The date is followed by a colon. A period is placed after the page number(s). If the article begins on one page but is continued on a non-consecutive page, a comma is inserted between the page numbers (e.g., 84, 97, 99). If the article appears on consecutive pages, a hyphen is inserted between the page numbers (e.g., 84–87).*

```
                                              6

   "Women in Math." Atlanta Journal-

   Constitution. March, 2004: 8E.

```

Note: *The above example illustrates an unsigned newspaper article. The punctuation remains the same.*

Math Fair Projects and Research Activities

Record the following information for a computer reference:

If referencing a magazine article from the computer, follow the format for writing a bibliography card for a magazine article.

If referencing an encyclopedia from the computer, follow the format for writing an encyclopedia bibliography card.

3
Frietag, Mark. "Golden Ratio." _Phi:_ _That Golden Number_. Internet. Available: http://www.coe.uga.edu/emt669/student. Folders/Frietag.Mark/Homepage/Golden Ratio/goldenratio.html. Nov. 4, 2002.

Note: Bibliography cards need to be made if dictionaries, audiotapes, videotapes, DVDs, television programs, movies, interviews, letters, surveys, or the Internet are used. Ask your teacher for assistance for the correct form in writing your bibliography cards.

Note Taking

Note taking is a shortcut for writing down information that has been read and needs to be remembered. Taking notes is a very important process when writing a research paper; one cannot expect to remember all that is read.

Some writers choose to take notes on note sheets such as the sample note sheet on page 46. Others decide to take notes on index cards or slips of paper, using a different card for each main idea. Here are some helpful hints for preparing note cards:

1. Write a word or phrase that summarizes the information on the top left-hand corner of the note card.

2. Write the number from the bibliography card that lists the source of the information used on the top right-hand corner of the note card.

3. Write the information on the note cards in your own words (paraphrase). Write only one idea per note card. Do not write notes from two sources on the same card.

4. If using quoted material, write the material enclosed in quotation marks. Limit the use of direct quotes when taking notes.

5. At the bottom of every note card, write the page number of the source in which the information was found.*

```
Pendulums                                    4

  Galileo researched pendulums to discover
  that only a change in the length of the
  string would change the behavior of the
  pendulum.


  page 16
```

*Adapted from *How To Write A Great Research Paper*, Incentive Publications, Nashville, TN.

45

Math Fair Projects and Research Activities

Sample Note Sheet

Name _____ Date _____

Source _____

Title of Source: _____

Author's Name: _____

Publisher: _____

Copyright Year: _____

Place of Publication: _____

Page Numbers: _____

Title of Research: _____

Write your notes IN YOUR OWN WORDS:

_____

_____

_____

_____

_____

_____

_____

_____

_____

_____

_____

_____

_____

If necessary, continue your notes on another sheet of paper.

Name _____

Note-Taking Practice

Use your judgment in choosing the most important and least important statements. Read the article carefully, then answer the questions that follow.

Probability Theory

Most of the early important work in probability theory was done by Fermat (1601–1665) and another French mathematician, Blaise Pascal (1623–1662). Some work had been done in this area before by the gambler-mathematician Girolamo Cardano (1501–1576), an Italian.

A gambler would have good reason to be interested in probability theory. This branch of mathematics is concerned with chance. It finds out what the chances are of one result happening out of a number of possible results. When a gambler uses dice or cards, he is interested in chance. For example, he may want to know his chances for rolling a 7 instead of a 10 with a pair of dice.

Probability theory is used not only to find betting odds, but also in daily weather reports to give the likelihood of rain. It is used in many other areas, such as science and business.

Therefore, one could say that probability deals with chances. For example, if you have 5 possible solutions to a situation, then the chance that one of them will happen is 1 out of 5. When using probability, the symbol for this is $\frac{1}{5}$. This symbol is a fraction and should be used like any fraction.

What if you were to toss a coin? Obviously there are two possible results. The coin can land tails up or heads up. The probability that the coin will land tails up is 1 out of 2 or $\frac{1}{2}$. The probability that it will land heads up is also $\frac{1}{2}$.

1. What is the probability of a coin landing tails up?

_____

_____

2. Who did the earlier important work in probability theory?

_____

_____

3. Name two of the three ways mentioned that probability can be used today.

_____

_____

4. Why would a gambler be interested in the probability theory?

_____

_____

Math Fair Projects and Research Activities

Name _____

Note-Taking Practice

When taking notes, begin by skimming the material in order to get a general idea of the content. When reading the material for the second time, read more carefully in order to find the main points and details. Instead of writing complete sentences, make brief notes.

On the right side of this page, take notes on the article below. Remember to use brief notes instead of complete sentences. Check the article for main ideas, cue words, and punctuation. Remember to use quotation marks for direct quotes.

Leonard Fibonacci	Notes
Leonard Fibonacci, who is responsible for introducing an essential tool for mathematical progress, lived in Pisa, Italy. He made a major contribution to the development of modern mathematics. Not much is known about his life except what he wrote in his best-known work, *Book of Calculations*. The publication of this book was a landmark in both the history of mathematics and the history of the Middle Ages. Fibonacci traveled around the Mediterranean Sea. He visited many places including Egypt, Syria, Sicily, and Constantinople. Everywhere he went he talked about mathematics. When he returned home, Leonard began to write about the new information he had learned. The purpose of his book was to introduce and explain the Hindu-Arabic numbers. Fibonacci included numerous examples of how Roman numerals could be translated into these new numbers. He also explained various operations that could be completed with these numbers. Fibonacci's most important achievement in number theory was what is known as a type of algebra called Diophantine analysis. This type of algebra deals with indeterminates, equations in two or more unknowns that require a solution using whole numbers or common fractions.	

Chapter Eight

CREATING AN OUTLINE

Creating an Outline

Creating an outline will make writing a research paper easier. Think of an outline as the "writing plan." An outline helps the writer sort out the main ideas and the supporting facts. The main ideas and supporting facts were recorded on the note cards during the research phase of the project. The outline will help plan the best order for those ideas.

1. Write the title of the paper across the top of the page.

2. Place a Roman numeral and a period before each main topic.

3. When dividing the main topic into subtopics, be sure to indent, placing the "A" directly underneath the first letter of the first word of the main topic.

4. If a main topic is divided, it must have at least two subtopics.

5. If using words or phrases instead of complete sentences in the outline, do not place a period after a main topic or subtopic.

6. Always begin the main topic and subtopic with a capital letter and capitalize any proper nouns.

7. An outline should use parallel structure. In other words, the same kind of word or phrase should be used.

> *Incorrect Use:* I. Travels of Leonard Fibonacci
> A. Around the Mediterranean Sea
> B. Communication

The example is incorrect because it does not use parallel structure consistently. The topic is a phrase, the first subtopic is a phrase, and the second subtopic is a single word. The following example shows an outline correctly written in phrases.

Careers in Mathematics

I. Mathematics in the Sciences
    A. Probability in biology
    B. Mathematical analysis in geology

II. Mathematics in Accounting
    A. Understanding of arithmetic
    B. Knowledge of business problems

III. Mathematics in Computer Programming
    A. Career as a programmer
    B. Career as a technician
    C. Career as a teacher

Math Fair Projects and Research Activities
Copyright ©2004 by Incentive Publications, Inc., Nashville, TN.

Outlining Practice

Read the following information, then complete the outline under the major headings on the following page.

The History of Algebra

Algebraic notation developed in three stages: rhetorical, syncopated, and symbolic. It developed over a period of 4,000 years. Because algebra developed from arithmetic, the introduction and use of irrational numbers, zero, negative numbers, and complex numbers is an integral part of its history.

A great deal of our understanding of mathematics from ancient Egypt, including algebra, comes from the Rhind papyrus. It was written about 1650 B.C. The Egyptians had the ability to solve problems that would be equivalent to linear equations using one unknown. The method that they used is now called the "false position" method. It was rhetorical or verbal because it did not use symbols.

The Cairo Papyrus, dated around 300 B.C. shows that Egyptians could solve some problems similar to using a system of equations in two unknowns. Without a doubt, the Egyptians were hampered by their difficult method of dealing with fractions.

The Babylonian's mathematical system was more advanced than the Egyptians' system. Since they had an exceptional numeration system, it led to an algebraic system that was highly developed. The Babylonians had a basic procedure that was equivalent to solving quadratic equations. They also used systems that were about the same as two equations in two unknowns.

Some symbols were used but not often. Their algebra was basically rhetorical like the Egyptians'. Examples were used to teach the methods for solving problems. They also only used positive rational numbers like the Egyptians.

During the classical period, the Greeks also did not recognize irrational numbers. They used the geometric form to prove and express a variety of algebraic identities and constructions that would be equivalent to the solution of quadratic equations. The Greeks' most important accomplishment was the way they described their procedures and their application of deductive reasoning.

Around A.D. 250 a Greek mathematician, Diophantus, introduced the syncopated style of writing equations. This was the result of a movement by other Greek mathematicians. Diophantus wrote his *Arithmetica* where he gave a treatment of indeterminate equations. Today these are known as "Diophantine equations." He used different methods for solving all of the 189 problems in the *Arithmetica*.

The Hindus used math in their study of astronomy and astrology. They used a base ten notation which was the standard used by 600 A.D. The Hindus discussed operations using zero, which they treated as a number. They used negative numbers to show debts. Proper procedures for using irrational numbers were also developed by the Hindus. Hindus used some symbols and stated the steps in the solutions of problems but with no reasons or proofs. The Hindus understood that quadratic equations had two roots. They included irrational and negative roots. Indeterminate quadratic equations were also considered by the Hindus.

51

Name _____

Outlining Practice

After reading the information about the history of algebra, complete the following outline.

I. Egyptian Algebra

    A. _____

        1._____

        2._____

        3._____

    B. _____

II. Babylonian Algebra

    A. More Advanced

        1._____

        2._____

    B. Like Egyptians

        1._____

        2._____

III. Greek Algebra

    A. _____

    B. _____

    C. _____

IV. Diophantine Algebra

    A. _____

    B. Arithmetica

        1._____

        2._____

V. Hindu Algebra

    A. _____

    B. _____

    C. Negative Numbers

    D. _____

    E. _____

    F. Quadratic Equations

        1._____

        2._____

Math Fair Projects and Research Activities   Copyright ©2004 by Incentive Publications, Inc., Nashville, TN.

Name _____

Outlining Practice

To further test your knowledge of outlines, parts of two outlines are given below. The outlines are in scrambled order. For the first outline (on the left), the form is supplied. For the second outline, create the form from scratch.

Importance
Assumptions
Perpendicular Lines
Basic Elements
Quadrilaterals
Definitions
Angle Bisection
Theorems
Triangles
Constructions

Suggestion: Place the Roman numerals first for each of the three main topics. Leave spaces for the subtopics under each main topic.

Measuring Size and Space	Tools
Systems	Length and Distance
Volume	Derived Measurements
Basic Measurements	Area
Making Measurements	Using Other Measurements

Geometry

Measurements

I. _____

II. Geometric Proof

    A. _____

    B. _____

    C. _____

    D. _____

III. _____

    A. _____

    B. Line Bisection

    C. _____

IV. Geometric Figures

    A. _____

    B. _____

Math Fair Projects and Research Activities

Chapter Nine

WRITING THE RESEARCH PAPER

Guidelines for the Research Paper

Upon the completion of your experiment, it is time to write the first draft of the research paper. When starting a first draft, concentrate only on putting the main ideas on paper. Do not be concerned with punctuation, grammar, or spelling. The following evaluation guidelines will help as you write your rough draft.

Title Page	Include project title, name, address, school, and grade.
Table of Contents	Number each section when writing is complete.
Introduction	The introduction should explain the background information concerning the topic and the reasons for the choice of study. Refer to previous research, as well as the project's experiments. Establish a strong rationale for the study by emphasizing unresolved issues or questions. Conclude by stating the research hypothesis.
Materials & Procedures	Describe in detail the methodology used to derive the data and observations. Use photographs and drawings of the equipment to describe your experiment further. Include a precise description of the sample, any apparatus that was constructed or modified for the study, and methods of data collection.
Results	Present the data collected in the experiment in tables and graphs. Summarize the data in narrative form. Include statistical analysis of the data. Do not include raw data. Include only information collected during the current year's study.
Discussion	The results and conclusion should flow smoothly and logically from the data. Be thorough. Compare results with theoretical values, published data, commonly held beliefs, and/or expected results. A complete paper should include a discussion of possible errors or problems experienced.
Conclusion	Briefly summarize the results. Discuss if the data supported the hypothesis and what the next steps in experimentation may be.

Math Fair Projects and Research Activities

Acknowledgements and Credits	Credit any assistance received from mentors, parents, teachers, and other sources.
Bibliography	The reference list should include any material that is found in outside sources (i.e, books, encyclopedias, websites, papers, journal articles, and communications cited in the paper). Follow the prescribed bibliographic recommendations in this book.
Appendix	Include critical information that is too lengthy for the main section of the paper, such as raw data, additional tables and graphs, copies of surveys and tests, and diagrams of specialized equipment.

Adapted from International Rules for Precollege Science Research: Guidelines for Science and Engineering Science Fairs, 2000–2001.

Here are examples of an introductory paragraph and conclusion:

Introductory Paragraph

Boolean algebra is a form of algebra in which functions and variables take on only one of the two values. This form of algebra has only two elements, zero and one, and is defined by different rules. Boolean algebra is the basis for digital logic, which is also the basis for computer design. This type of algebra can be used in many ways; however, in this paper the main ways will be addressed.

Conclusion

From my research, one might conclude that Boolean algebra is an abstract mathematical system. It is used in computer science and in expressing the relationship between sets. Its use with modern digital computers is a natural one. Using Boolean algebra in the searching process is advantageous because it narrows the field of information necessary for research.

Writing the Abstract

Abstracts, which are concise summaries of articles or books, routinely precede articles in journals and in certain periodical or bibliographic guides. Abstracts can help a reader decide whether or not to read the entire work. In the case of your math research project, you may be required to write an abstract.

The following rules are based on those from the International Rules for Precollege Science Research: Guidelines for Science Fairs, sponsored by Science Services, Inc., Washington, D.C.

- The abstract must be typed.
- Using all capitals, type the title, student name, district fair, and category.
- The abstract should be 250 words or less.
- The abstract **should** include the following:

  a) purpose of the experiment   c) data   e) any possible research application
  b) procedures used   d) conclusion   f) minimal reference to previous work

- The abstract **should not** include
  a) acknowledgements
  b) work or procedures completed by someone other than the student.

The following is an example of an abstract:

TITLE: *Which Games Are Fair?*

NAME: Brian Spencer

REGIONAL FAIR: DEKALB/ROCKDALE SCIENCE & MATHEMATICS FAIR

CATEGORY: Mathematics

The purpose of this experiment was to determine the fairness of the "Red versus Blue" game. The experimental procedures were as follows:

- Place the same number of red and blue cubes in a bag.
- A red team and a blue team take turns reaching into the bag without looking, removing one cube, examining and recording its color, and replacing it.
- Teams record their scores, placing a tally mark on a tally sheet.
- Teams play a predetermined number of rounds as a test to determine if the game is fair.
- The winner is the team that has drawn the most cubes matching their team color—red or blue.

Results showed a fifty-fifty chance of getting either a red or blue cube, thus the game was fair. To further explore probability, I varied the number of red or blue cubes, i.e., three blue cubes and one red cube. I asked teams to predict whether the new games where variations of cubes were used were fair or not. Teams played the game and used the results to confirm or modify their predictions. Teams constructed tree diagrams showing all outcomes for the game to determine fairness.

Math Fair Projects and Research Activities

Name _____

Introductory Paragraph Practice

While writing the introductory paragraph, keep in mind that the introduction should include background information and the reasons for the choice of study. Conclude by stating the hypothesis.

Directions: Edit the first draft paragraph. While rewriting the paragraph, feel free to change any of the words, place the sentences in a more logical order, and remove any sentences that do not agree with the main topic. Also correct any errors in spelling, capitalization, and punctuation.

His research, centered around things that would affect the timing of a pendulum's swing. Pendullums are used in time measurment as well as musical measurement. In the past, they have been used to detect earthquakers and also to measure the strength of gravity. Galileo galilei became fascinated with pendulums and researched its behavior. Galileo was forced to leave the University of Pisa in 1585! From Galileo's research he found that the only thing that would change a pendulum's behavior was a change in the length of the string. Were Galileo's Experiments accurate and how are pendulums still used in today's society?

_____

_____

_____

_____

_____

_____

_____

_____

_____

Conclusion Practice

Remember that the concluding paragraph should briefly summarize results. It should include discussion of whether or not the data supported the hypothesis. Finally, include what the next steps in experimentation may be.

Directions: Read the following conclusion. Feel free to change any of the words, place the sentences in a more logical order, and remove any sentences that do not agree with the main topic. Also, correct any errors in spelling, capitalization, and punctuation.

It is amazing that one simple number can shape our world, It is the length between the mathamatical world and the human perciption of perfection. The Golden Ratio continues to open doors in our understanding of life and the universe. The thorax and the abdomen in most bees is nearly equal to the golden ratio. For the last several thousand years, the Golden Ratio has captured the interest and wonder of humankind and it still has not lost its touch. people every day are still seeking for the treasures that are yet found in the Golden Ratio? When think we have discovered and understand all the little hidden secrets of the Divine Proportion, it turns up and surprises us in a unexpectted places

_____

_____

_____

_____

_____

_____

_____

_____

_____

_____

Math Fair Projects and Research Activities

Name _____

Abstract Practice

When writing your abstract, remember that an abstract is a concise summary of the entire research project. It should include the following: purpose, hypothesis, procedure, data, conclusions, and possible applications.

Directions: Edit the following abstract. While rewriting the abstract, feel free to change any of the words, place the sentences in a more logical order, and remove any sentences that do not agree with the main topic. Also, correct any errors in spelling, capitalization, and punctuation.

We recorded the time needed for the vertical descent of the Arrow during each shot or drop. The purpose of this experiment was to study the behavior of a Nerf-gun arrow under two different conditions: dropped and fired horizontally! Our team attempted to prove that the two arrows will use the same amount of time to descend to the ground. After several trials. the team recorded their experimentation of several varying heights of fireing and droping our arrows. Shooting Nerf-guns is fun! After graphical and experimental comparisons of the data, we found the arrow to indicate the results we expected. analyzing the data indicated that horizontal velocity acted upon the arrow separate from gravitational pull.

_____

_____

_____

_____

_____

_____

_____

_____

_____

_____

Name _____

Writing the Introductory Paragraph

Directions: In the space provided, write an introductory paragraph. If needed, continue writing the first draft on your notebook paper.

_____

Title of the Math Research Paper

Introductory Paragraph: _____

_____

_____

_____

_____

_____

_____

_____

_____

_____

_____

_____

_____

_____

_____

_____

Name _____

Writing the Conclusion

Directions: In the space provided, write your conclusion. Remember that the conclusion
can be one or two paragraphs. Briefly summarize your results. Discuss
whether the data supported the hypothesis, and what the next steps in
experimentation may be.

Conclusion: _____

_____

_____

_____

_____

_____

_____

_____

_____

_____

_____

_____

_____

_____

_____

_____

Name _____

Writing the Abstract

Directions: In the space provided, write an abstract. Remember to finish the research and experimentation before writing the abstract. An abstract, a concise summary of the entire research project, should be completed in 250 words or less.

Title: _____

Name: _____

Regional Fair: _____

Category: _____

_____

_____

_____

_____

_____

_____

_____

_____

_____

_____

_____

_____

_____

_____

_____

Math Fair Projects and Research Activities

Chapter Ten

PREPARING THE FINAL BIBLIOGRAPHY

Preparing the Final Bibliography

In Chapter 7, "Bibliography Cards and Note Taking," the student learned how to create bibliography cards for the sources used to write a research paper (books, encyclopedias, pamphlets, films, newspaper and magazine articles, interviews, lectures, letters, and the Internet). Those cards will be helpful when creating a final bibliography.

When making the bibliography list:

1) include all sources used for completing the project,

2) put the list in alphabetical order according to the author's last name (if the author is not given, alphabetize by the first word in the title),

3) underline the title of books, encyclopedias, newspapers, and magazines, and

4) record the city, publishing company, and date of publication.

Place the bibliography after the acknowledgement page of a research paper.

Each final bibliographical entry should resemble the following examples:

Book with a single author:

Freilig, Mark. <u>Leonard of Pisa</u>. New York: Workman Publishing Company, 1990.

Book with more than one author:

Cantor, David and Melissa Kasner. <u>The Fundamental Mathematics</u>. Philadelphia: McCoy Publishing Company, 2002.

Book with an editor:

Poole, Ann, ed. <u>Applications of the Pythagorean Theorem</u>. New York: Harcourt Publishing, 1992.

Pamphlet:

"Egyptian Fractions." <u>The Secrets of the Pyramids</u>. London, England: The Royal Mathematics Council, 1989

Math Fair Projects and Research Activities

Magazine with an author listed:

Koch, Julia. "What's the Truth about Morley's Triangle?" <u>Mathematics Today</u>. November, 1999: 7–12.

Newspaper article—unsigned:

"Democritus." <u>Los Angles Times</u>. Dec. 3, 2000, Sec. D, p. 12.

Encyclopedia with a signed article:

Mertz, Barbara. "Pyramids." <u>The World Book Encyclopedia</u>. 2000.

Encyclopedia article—unsigned:

"Golden Section." <u>Funk & Wagnalls New Encyclopedia</u>. 1998 ed.

Television program:

"What Fractal Dimension?" Discovery Channel. Adrien-Marie Weierstrass. April 3, 1999.

Accessed through a computer service:

"The Abacus." <u>Periodical Abstracts</u>. Online. Galileo. 12 June 1987.

Periodically published database on CD-ROM:

Gardner, Casey. "Kaleidoscope." <u>Using Math in Everyday Objects</u>. April 12, 2002: 17–21. CD-ROM. Spring, 2002.

Publication on a diskette:

Newton, Victor. "Fibonacci Numbers." Diskette. Houston: Edward Graham Publishing Company, 1997.

Writing Bibliographical Entries

When writing a research paper, it is necessary to include a bibliography at the end. The bibliography is a list of all the sources used when gathering information for the paper. Bibliographies follow a special format and list important information about each source. Write bibliographical entries for the sources listed below. As a guide, refer to pages 65–66.

1. A book called <u>Addition and Subtraction</u> was written by Abbey Cuss and published by Model Publishing Company, of Countville, in 1999.

   _____

   _____

2. "Using Pi" written by Di Ameter was found Online and published by Area Publishers in Circle City, on May 13, 2001.

   _____

   _____

3. A pamphlet entitled <u>Using Equations</u> by Lyn E. Er was produced by The Vari Able Publishing Corporation in Algebratown in 2003.

   _____

   _____

4. Appearing in Vol. 15 of <u>Theorem Encyclopedia</u> in 1999 was an article on "The Pythagorean Theorem" written by Hypot E. Nuse and found on pages 201–211.

   _____

   _____

Math Fair Projects and Research Activities

5. Published by Mandelbrot Sets Publishing of Koch Curve City, Snow Flake wrote an article entitled "Drawing Fractals" for Simple Equations Magazine in December of 1999.

_____

_____

6. Noisy Times contained an article in Section D, page 3 on "Parabolic Reflector Microphones" written by S. P. Orting Events and produced by Sound Publishers on January 21, 1995.

_____

_____

7. A book on Galileo Galilei was jointly written by Johannes Kepler and P. Tolemy and published by Pendulum Brothers, Pisa, Italy in 1995.

_____

_____

8. P. L. Atonic was interviewed by Archi Median at 10:00 A.M. on June 17, 2001 in Solid Falls, Vermont.

_____

9. I received an email through Mathmet, entitled "Card Tricks" on July 4, 2003. Persi Diaconis wrote it on June 30, 2003. It was then received from statisticiansgroup.comp. magic.tricks

_____

_____

Math Fair Projects and Research Activities   68

Bibliography Practice

Julian really needs help writing a bibliographic list. He used the sources listed in the paragraph below while writing his math research paper: "The Golden Ratio." For the bibliography, use the lines below.

In the book <u>Golden Ratio</u> by Joseph Wassermann, Paul Robert Trumble, and Barbara Nelson-Klein, Julian found the information. The book was published by Wolfram Publishing Company in Hanover, in 1999. He also found an article entitled "Fibonacci Sequence" in <u>World Book Encyclopedia</u> produced by Childcraft International, Inc. in 1993. The third source was the book <u>Phi: That Golden Number</u> written by Isabelle Frances Peterson in 2002 and published by Greg & Collins Publishing of Atlanta. He found an article entitled <u>Harrison's Golden Ratio Extravaganza</u> on the Internet at http://biology.mathforum.worldofmath/uga.edu/page3/html. Finally, Julian located an article entitled "Using Golden Ratio" in the <u>Encyclopedia Britannica</u>, Vol. 8, pages 112–118. It was published in 2003.

Bibliography

_____

_____

_____

_____

_____

_____

_____

_____

_____

_____

_____

_____

Math Fair Projects and Research Activities

Writing the Final Bibliography

It is now time to write a rough draft bibliography. Use the space provided below. Remember to follow these steps:

1) Put the list in alphabetical order according to the author's last name (if the author is not given, alphabetize by the first word in the title);

2) Underline the title of books, encyclopedias, newspapers, and magazines;

3) Record the city, publishing company and date of publication. If needed, refer to pages 65–66.

Bibliography

_____

_____

_____

_____

_____

_____

_____

_____

_____

_____

_____

_____

Chapter Eleven

DATA REPRESENTATION

Data Representation

The way in which you display the results of your research will enhance the visual appeal of your mathematics project. Graphing is one way to organize data so that people can easily and quickly interpret its meaning. Graphs add color to the backboard and provide evidence of your hard work in researching the topic.

There are many kinds of charts and graphs to choose from when selecting a format for data. Some common ways to display data are pie graphs, line graphs, bar graphs, and pictographs.

The following section will discuss the most common types of graphs and give examples of each:

Pie Graphs

A pie graph is generally a circle that has been divided into sections to represent the results of research. Data is usually presented as a percentage of the total, or 100 percent. Pie graphs show percentages at a set point in time. They do not show changes over time.

To use a pie graph, a value must be assigned to each slice of the pie. Also, a name must be given to each slice, and a title created. Look at the example below.

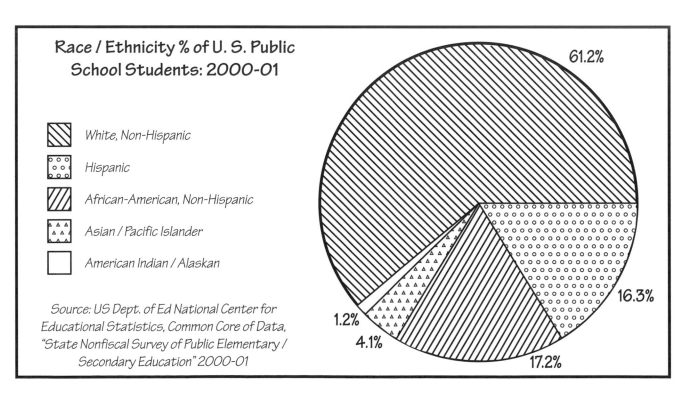

Race / Ethnicity % of U. S. Public School Students: 2000-01

White, Non-Hispanic

Hispanic

African-American, Non-Hispanic

Asian / Pacific Islander

American Indian / Alaskan

Source: US Dept. of Ed National Center for Educational Statistics, Common Core of Data, "State Nonfiscal Survey of Public Elementary / Secondary Education" 2000-01

61.2%

16.3%

17.2%

4.1%

1.2%

Line Graphs

A line graph shows the amount of change over a certain period of time. A line graph has a horizontal axis (x) and a vertical axis (y). One axis shows the length of time and the other axis shows the amount of change.

When creating a line graph, make it as simple or as complex as you wish. Look at the example below.

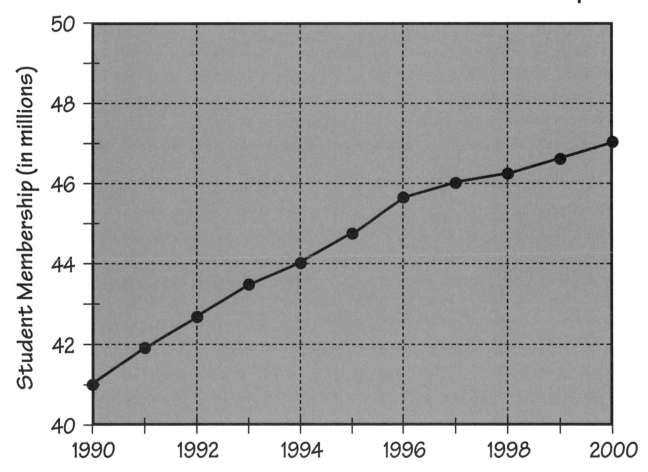

U. S. Public School Student Membership

The above graph of U.S. Public School Student Membership shows that student membership has increased from 41 million students in 1990 to 47 million students in 2000. At a glance, you can see that there was a steady rise in membership each year from 1990 to 2000.

Math Fair Projects and Research Activities

Bar Graphs

Bar graphs can be used to show how something changes over time or to compare items. A bar graph has a horizontal axis (x) and a vertical axis (y). Typically, the x-axis has values representing the time period or what is being measured. The vertical axis (y) has values for the amount of items being measured. A bar graph is an excellent way to show data that spans many days, weeks, months, or years, or changes over time. Also, the bar graph may be used to compare things. Bar graphs can be drawn vertically or horizontally. Look at the examples below:

Vertical representation:

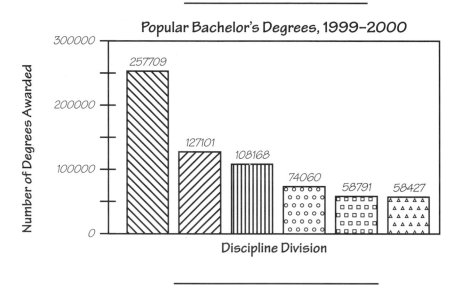

Horizontal representation:

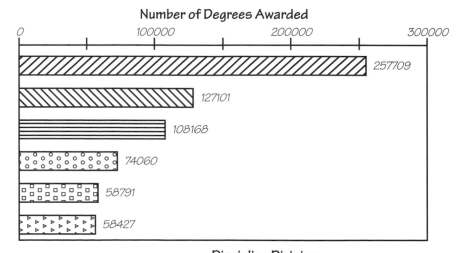

Discipline Division

Pictographs

In a pictograph, a picture or symbol is used to represent a number. The key or legend tells how many units are represented by each symbol, while the title communicates the subject of the graph. A pictograph uses pictures that are the same size to show information clearly. Look at the example below:

The Number of Hours Children Spent Reading Per Week

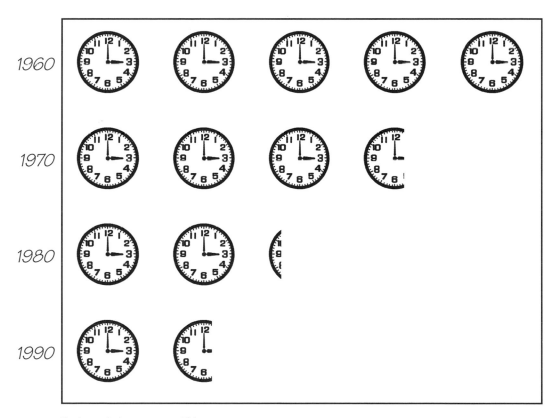

Each symbol represents 10 hours.

The pictograph shows that students in the 1960s spent 50 hours per week reading books while students in the 1990s spent only 15 hours a week reading.

Graphs adapted from the following website:
http://www.nces.ed.gov/nceskids/

Math Fair Projects and Research Activities

Sharpen Your Graphing Skills

A **bar graph** shows relationships between groups. It is a fast way to show big differences. The two items being compared do not need to affect each other.

1. John used different types of fertilizer on his bean crop to determine if there was a difference in growth with each brand used. His results are listed in the chart below. Draw a bar graph to represent his results. Give the bar graph a title. Label the horizontal axis (x) and the vertical axis (y).

BRAND OF FERTILIZER	AVERAGE HEIGHT IN CM
Granny's Choice	28.0
Jobe's House Plant Spikes	14.7
Miracle Gro	8.4
K Mart Fertilizer	22.4
No Fertilizer	13.0

Directions: On a separate sheet of paper, draw a bar graph to represent the data given in the above table.

A **line graph** shows continuing data—how one thing is affected by another. It is clear to see how things are progressing by the rising and falling of the line on the graph. This kind of graph is needed to show the effect of an independent variable on a dependent variable.

2. Jean compared the pulse rate of Mabel, a 36-year-old office worker and Albert, a 26-year-old college athlete. She collected the following data on each subject as they exercised for 5 minutes.

HEART RATE OVER FIVE MINUTES

Mabel	64	79	144	94	80
Albert	80	94	112	110	64

Directions: Draw a line graph to represent the pulse rate in beats per minute and the time in minutes for each subject. Be sure to give the line graph a title.

A **circle graph**, or **pie graph**, is used to show how a part of something relates to the whole. This kind of graph is needed to show percentages effectively.

3. Harriet surveyed her math class to find out her classmates' favorite flavors of ice cream. Her results are listed below:

ICE CREAM FLAVOR	PERCENTAGE OF STUDENTS
Vanilla	21%
Chocolate	33%
Strawberry	12%
Raspberry	4%
Peach	7%
Neopolitan	17%
Other	6%

Directions: Using the percentages from the chart, draw a pie graph. Each flavor of ice cream represents a "slice" of the pie graph. Label each slice, draw a key, and select a title.

Math Fair Projects and Research Activities

Chapter Twelve

SAMPLE MATHEMATICS RESEARCH PAPER

Sample Mathematics Research Paper

Now it is time to write the final draft of your mathematics fair research paper. Before beginning to handwrite or type the paper, remember that the final paper must be complete and neatly organized. Have you thought about using a computer to compose your math fair research paper? The computer, which will save you a great deal of time, allows one to save and retrieve the document. It will also allow for editing or making corrections quickly and easily. In this final stage, proofreading is crucial. Check for spelling, punctuation, capitalization, organization, clarity, word choice, and parallel structure.

When preparing the final draft, consider the following guidelines:

1. If handwriting the research paper, use lined paper.

2. Use blue or black pen.

3. Do not skip lines if writing on lined paper; however, when typing a paper, double-space it.

4. For both typing and handwriting, allow one inch for the top, bottom, left, and right margins.

5. The beginning of each paragraph should always be indented.

6. When preparing a title page, remember to include the title of the paper, the subject, your name, the teacher's name, your school, and the date.

7. Number the pages consecutively at the bottom center of each page (except the first page).

8. A research paper should be organized as follows: title page, table of contents, outline (if required), introductory paragraph(s), materials and procedures, results, discussion, conclusion, credits, bibliography, and appendix (if applicable).

9. Do not discard any materials (bibliography cards, outline, note cards, or drafts) because the teacher may ask for these items as well.

Math Fair Projects and Research Activities

On the following pages, there is a sample of the final typewritten mathematics research paper of Michelle Brouner and Sara Levy's project, *Useful Skills for Mental Arithmetic,* which won first place in Georgia's Mathematics Fair of 2001. The marginal notes have been added to assist you.

Title Page

The title page contains 1) the title of the mathematics research paper, 2) the name of the student, 3) the name of the school, 4) the teacher's name, 5) the grade level, and 6) the date due.

Title of paper, typed and centered on the page

Students' names

Name of school, teacher's name, grade level, and date due

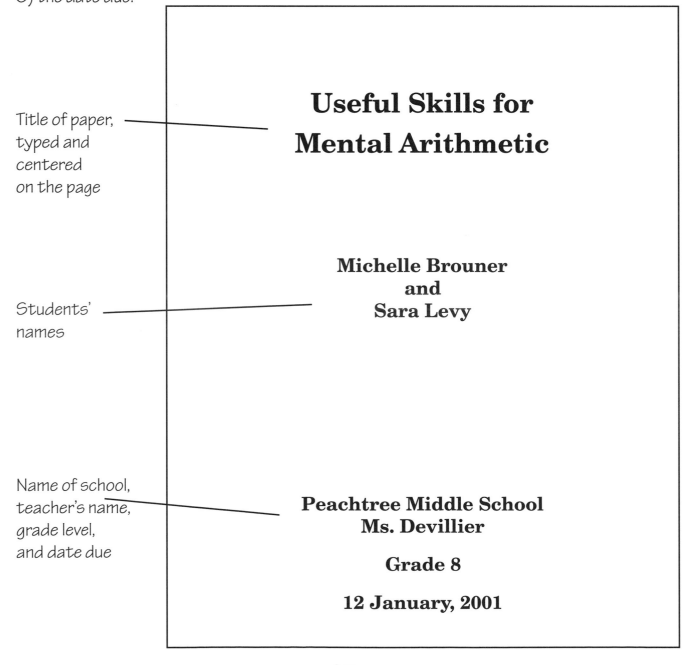

Useful Skills for Mental Arithmetic

**Michelle Brouner
and
Sara Levy**

**Peachtree Middle School
Ms. Devillier**

Grade 8

12 January, 2001

Abstract

Title	USEFUL SKILLS FOR MENTAL ARITHMETIC
Name	Michelle Brouner and Sara Levy
GSEF Regional Fair	DeKalb/Rockdale Counties
Category:	Mathematics

Abstract

There are many different types of teaching methods. Some of them are to teach toward the left or the right side of the brain, use games, or use visual aids. We taught a group of accelerated students at Chesnut Elementary School in DeKalb County School System. They were taught useful skills for mental arithmetic with a variety of teaching methods. Divisibility with the numbers 1–11 with the exception of 7, multiplying by 2, 4, 5, 10, and 11, adding fractions, converting fractions to decimals, and squaring numbers that end in 5 were the skills that the students were taught. The skills allowed the students to solve math problems more easily. The results of a posttest compared to the results of a pretest showed that these skills do help the students.

Centered
and typed

Table of Contents

Page

Notice all
required
parts
are
included.

Notice each
section indicates
the beginning
page number.

Title of paper is centered.

Paragraphs are properly indented.

Introduction: Reasons for mental math

Note that the background information is appropriately given.

Useful Skills for Mental Arithmetic

Mental arithmetic is an important aspect of math. It allows people to work problems in a quick and easy way. The more skills one knows, the more mental arithmetic one will be able to accomplish. Mental arithmetic can be taught in a variety of ways, and there are many skills which allow them to be incorporated into many lessons of all grade levels.

There are many different methods of teaching. A common style is to direct activities toward the left or right side of the brain depending on the students. Students who have a prominent left side learn better by ordering, analyzing, computing, and relying on proven practices. Students with a more prominent right side learn better by acting, experimenting, designing, inventing, and building models.

Worksheets, which are a visual aid that can help students to fully understand a topic, are often used as a reference. Overhead projectors also serve this purpose. In addition, students tend to concentrate more when an overhead is being used in a dark classroom. When the only light is coming from the overhead, students will usually look up at that light source. Games frequently stimulate and interest students. They allow them to have fun while learning main ideas. Other strategies include hands-on activities,

- 4 -

83

brainstorming, manipulatives, creative ideas, graphic organizers, and Bloom's Taxonomy.

In the 2000–2001 school year, fifth grade students will learn about area and perimeter, Roman numerals, ratios, and estimation. The students will also learn about Polyominos, which are patterns of squares where all of the squares that touch each other share at least one side. Addition, subtraction, multiplication, and division of decimals will be taught as well as prime factorization and least common multiples. Other areas included in the curriculum (for particular students) are problem solving, probability, the metric system, geometry, and pre-algebra concepts, such as variables and integers.

An experiment will be conducted on a Discovery/Impact (gifted) fifth grade class. The experiment will show the usefulness of these skills. A variety of skills for mental arithmetic will be taught. Many of them are shortcuts to see if a number is divisible by another number with no remainders. If a number is divisible by 2, the last digit will be an even number. If a number is divisible by 3, then the sum of all of the digits will be divisible by 3. In order for a number to be divisible by 4, 4 will go evenly into the last 2 digits. For example, in the number 652, 52 is divisible by 4 so 652 is divisible by 4. If a number ends in a 5 or a 0, it is divisible by 5. A number that is divisible by both 2 and 3 will also

- 5 -

Additional background information is given here.

Notice that the description of the experiment has been included.

Rules of
divisibility

Shortcuts
for
multiplication

be divisible by 6. The skill for the number 8 is similar to the skill for the number 4 except that for a number to be divisible by 8 its last three digits must be divisible by 8. The skill for the number 9 is much more like the skill for 3, but the sum of the digits has to be divisible by 9. One can easily find out if a number is divisible by 11. To do this, start from the right side and place a subtraction sign between the last two digits. Then place an addition sign between the second to last and the third to last digits. Continue alternating between addition and subtraction until the end of the number. Work the problem just created from right to left. If the answer is 11 or 0, then the number is divisible by 11.

There are also shortcuts for multiplication. When one multiplies a number by 2, simply double it. If one is multiplying a number by 4, it will be easier if you double it and then double it again. When you multiple a number by 10, add a zero at the end of the number. To multiple by 5, add a 0 to the end of the number and then divide by 2. There is also a skill for multiplying by 11. In a two-digit number, it will be necessary to write the two digits. Then add the two digits together and place the sum in between the two digits. This is the product. For example, in the number 52, 5 plus 2 equals 7; therefore, the product is 572. In the number 97, do the same thing except

- 6 -

Discussion continues on shortcuts for multiplication

Note that an answer is presented.

Note the paragraph has been properly indented.

Shortcuts for fractions

do not write down the number 1. Nine plus seven equals 16; carry the 1 over and add it to the 9, and then the final answer is 1,067. When multiplying a three-digit number by 11, write the first and last digits. Next, add the last two digits together and write the sum in front of the last digit. Finally, add the first two digits and place the sum after the first digit. For instance, in the number 423, write the 4 and 3. Next, add the 3 and the 2 and write the sum in front of the 3. Add the 4 and the 2 and place the sum after the 4. The final answer will be 4,653. If carrying is needed, it follows the same rule as when multiplying 11 by a two-digit number. For larger numbers, continue to add the digits that are next to each other, placing the sum in the proper position.

One shortcut for fractions involves changing fractions to decimals, and another shortcut involves adding fractions. If there is a number less than 9 over 9, that number will be the repeating decimal when converting fractions to decimals. For instance, 2/9 will convert into $.\overline{2}$. If a number less than 99 is over 99, then it will be the repeating decimal. If it is a single digit number, place a 0 in front of it. The same thing applies for fractions with a different amount of 9s in the denominator, with the amount of digits and zeros needed for the numerator changing accordingly. If there is a fraction that is not an

- 7 -

Shortcuts for fractions continued

improper fraction with 11 as the denominator, multiply the numerator and the denominator by 9 to make it a fraction over 99. Now convert the fraction into a decimal. The shortcut to add fractions makes it so that finding a common denominator is unnecessary. Cross multiply and add the two products. This is the numerator. Multiply the two denominators to find the final denominator.

Shortcut for squaring numbers

There is a shortcut for squaring numbers that end in 5. The answer will end in 25. Multiply the numeral before the 5 and the next consecutive number (1 + numeral before the 5). For example, when squaring 15, the answer will end in 25. Next, multiply 1 times 2. The final answer will be 225.

All teachers must find their own effective method of teaching. These methods allow them to express their point of utilizing visual aids and/or oral communication. They must be used to teach the skills for mental arithmetic. Fifth grade students can use the skills in much of their work. These skills are also good to use on timed tests, such as the Iowa Test of Basic Skills. The teaching methods will be an important part of the experiment. They will need to be used to make sure that the students understand the skills.

Project proposal

For our project, Useful Skills for Mental Arithmetic, we are going to teach fifth grade Discovery/Impact (gifted) class

Page number centered

- 8 -

Project proposal continued

at Chesnut Elementary. The materials that we will need to complete our project will be a backboard, a camera, an overhead projector, transparencies, overhead markers, and assorted construction paper. Our plan is to teach the students useful skills for mental arithmetic. In order to teach mental arithmetic, we plan to use an overhead projector and visuals.

We will administer a timed mental arithmetic pretest. This test will be graded to determine the students' weaknesses and strengths. Next, we will teach the students the shortcut skills in multiplication, divisibility, fractions, and squaring numbers. Students will be able to ask questions throughout the lesson. Handouts will be distributed so that students can follow along with the transparencies.

When we have completed teaching the various skills and feel that the students have comprehended them, we will then administer a posttest. A comparison will be made of the test results to determine our effectiveness in teaching mental arithmetic.

Results of the experiment

On arrival at Chesnut Elementary, we introduced ourselves and explained our mental arithmetic project to the fifth-grade students. First, we administered a pretest covering the material that we were planning to teach. When the students finished, they raised their hands,

- 9 -

*Results
of the
experiment
continued*

and we recorded the amount of time needed for each student to complete the test. Next, we distributed the divisibility handout and began to teach this math skill.

We alternated teaching each skill. A copy of the handout which was on the overhead was used. Many examples were shown, and the students were allowed to ask any questions. The same procedure was followed for the multiplication and fractions/squaring handouts. After we finished teaching the skills, we did a quick review.

To make sure that the students understood the skills, we played a game. The class was divided into two teams. One person from each team would go to the board. They were given a problem, and the first person with the correct answer was awarded a point. If neither person answered correctly, the student was able to receive help from the team. Following each point, we explained how the problem was supposed to be solved.

When we thought the students were comfortable with the skills, we administered the posttest. It was actually the same as the pretest. When the students finished, we recorded their times. We also noted whether or not they used the skills on the test. We noted that most of the students had used the skills on the posttest.

- 10 -

Conclusion

After comparing the results of the posttest to those of the pretest, we concluded that the skills that were taught are very useful. Almost all of the students used the skills and made an improvement. When the students first learned the skills, they were unsure about their ability to use them accurately. The more the students practiced using the skills, the more comfortable they became. When they took the pretest, the students worked all the problems on paper; however, on the posttest most of the students calculated the answers in their heads. Overall, the results show that the mental arithmetic skills were effective in improving test scores.

Graph of test results

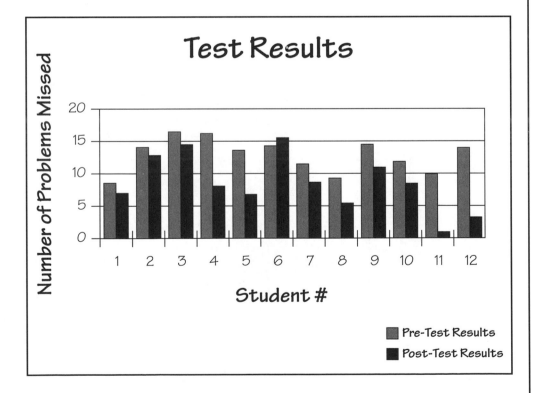

- 11 -

90

Centered ———————————————— **Bibliography**

Bzuk, Nadine S. and Harry Bohan. *Houghton Mifflin Mathematics.* Boston: Houghton Mifflin Company, 1995.

Calvert, Sarah. Interviewed in Atlanta, Georgia. October 27, 2000.

Edwards, Marsha. Interviewed in Atlanta, Georgia. November 9, 2000.

K–12 Math Problems, Puzzles, Tips and Tricks. The Math Forum:@Drexel. http://mathforum.org/k12/mathtips

Kellogg, Robert. Interviewed in Atlanta, Georgia. November 11, 2000.

Entries in alphabetical order

Marshall, Scott. Interviewed in Atlanta, Georgia. September 29, 2000.

Multiplying 3 Digits or More by 11. CuriousMath.com http://www.curiousmath.com

Prindle, Anthony and Katie Prindle. *Math The Easy Way.* 3rd ed. New York: Barron's Educational Series, Inc., 1996.

Spector, Lawrence. *The Meaning of Multiplication: Mental Arithmetic.* The Math Page. http://the_mathpage.com/index.html

- 12 -

Math Fair Projects and Research Activities

Appendix

Pretest/Posttest

Name _____ **Date** _____

Directions: Answer the following questions in the time given.

Of 2, 3, 5, 6, 9, and 10 list which numbers each number below is divisible by:

1. 126 _____   3. 1,521 _____

2. 513 _____   4. 120,128 _____

Multiply:

5. 5 x 13 _____   7. 2 x 27 _____

6. 4 x 83 _____   8. 11 x 12 _____

Write each fraction as a decimal:

9. $\frac{2}{5}$ _____   11. $\frac{3}{10}$ _____

10. $\frac{7}{8}$ _____   12. $\frac{3}{4}$ _____

Add:

13. $\frac{5}{6} + \frac{1}{12}$ _____   15. $\frac{1}{6} + \frac{3}{4}$ _____

14. $\frac{3}{8} + \frac{5}{16}$ _____   16. $\frac{1}{2} + \frac{1}{3}$ _____

Square the following numbers:

17. 15^2 _____   19. 35^2 _____

18. 25^2 _____   20. 45^2 _____

- 13 -

PREPARING THE BACKBOARD

How to Begin a Backboard

1. Begin gathering materials early for the backboard. Save everything: copies of every letter written requesting information about your topic: magazine articles, newspaper articles, emails, photographs, pamphlets. Use a basket, drawer, or box to collect and save these items. Remember: Never discard anything until you have completed your project.

2. Buy or build the backboard. (Backboards may be purchased from the local office or school supply store.) If you are making your backboard, you may purchase supplies from your local hardware store.

3. Backboards may be covered with fabric or paper, painted, or purchased in various colors.

4. Create a drawing of your backboard plan. Be sure to include the required parts of a backboard (see example on page 95). Try several sketches or plans and choose the one that best suits your purpose. Keep in mind that an orderly arrangement will bring unity to the work, and that a preliminary sketch will help work out problems on paper.

5. If required, submit your final drawing to your teacher for approval.

6. Once approved, use the plan to lay out the letters and other items gathered on the backboard. Be sure to leave neat margins and good spacing for your letters.

7. Ask someone to check your lettering for correct spelling! Glue the letters and other documents to the backboard.

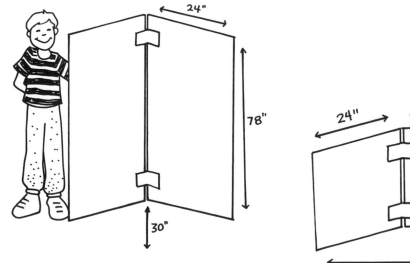
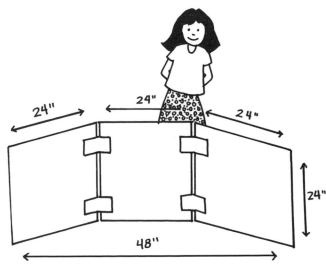

What Type of Backboard Should be Used?

The backboard should be made of sturdy materials, such as plywood, pegboard, cardboard, or another material. Commercially prepared foam core or cardboard backboards (pre-folded for easy use) can be found at art, office, or school supply stores. The backboard should be no larger than 48" in width, 78" in height, and 30" in depth. If desired, headers are also available. See the illustration below for the correct use of a backboard.

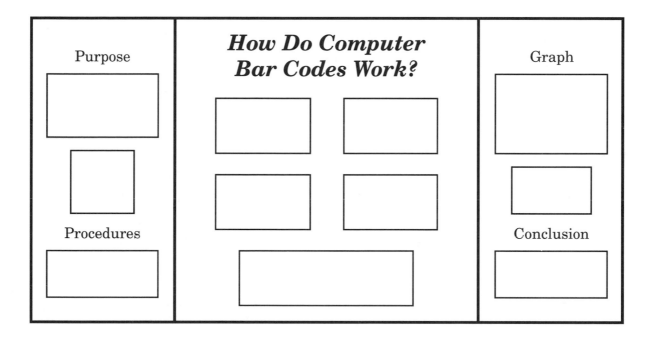

Advantages to Covering the Backboard

The color of the backboard should be part of the overall color scheme and should help reinforce the topic. A covered board should not fight the surface of the display board itself. For example, the grain of the wood, the texture of the circles in the pegboard, or the lines in the cardboard may compete with the design for attention. The background should be a part of the design and not something that works against it. Remember: A covered board should help to bring unity to the display.

Materials for Covering the Backboard

Painting the backboard will work well, especially on plywood. Make sure the paint is not too thin or watery. Felt or fabric that is not too thin can be used to cover your backboard. If you prefer, craft paper may also be used to cover a backboard. A variety of colors is usually available. Finally, why not consider using a colorful border for the backboard? These borders are available in a wide variety of designs at the local art, office, or school supply store.

Math Fair Projects and Research Activities

Decorating the Backboard

The materials for the backboard will depend on what is being illustrated. For example, use something as different as a fishing net if your topic calls for it. Try to be creative and use materials that will catch the eye of your audience and support the topic.

Design Elements

What design elements will make the backboard more attractive? An exceptional backboard, a work of art in itself, reflects good composition and orderly arrangement. The following principles of design will help to create good composition:

Center of Interest: Is there something that catches the eye? A center of interest draws a viewer's attention.

Color Scheme: The use of a color scheme will help organize the backboard. The colors chosen may reflect the topic. For example, red, white, and blue for a political theme; pastels for a feminine issue; black and yellow for strong visual clarity; shades of blue for a marine topic; and black or white (with another color) always makes a strong statement.

Contrast: Is there enough of a difference between the chosen colors to make for easy reading? You do not want your work to fade into the background.

Balance: Check to see that the overall design is carried throughout the backboard. Try to make groups of items evenly distributed so that harmony is achieved.

Variety: Are the graphs, charts, maps, diagrams, timelines, or pictures interesting to the viewer?

Rhythm: An orderly progression is important to good composition. Since people read from left to right, it is advisable to place the purpose to the left of the board and to end with the conclusion on the right. Give the backboard a sense of order, and it will be more easily read and understood by the viewer.

Unity: Does the backboard work with all the parts coming together as a whole? A backboard will achieve unity if all the parts are necessary. Do not overdo your project! Make the work clear and concise.

Avoiding Backboard Pitfalls

1. Avoid using correction fluid—it draws attention to the mistake.

2. Use spray fixatives in a well-vented area. White glue will wrinkle the paper, and once it is used, it has no "give" for repositioning letters or pictures.

3. Use straight pins to place materials prior to gluing. Items can still be rearranged, but the pins will prevent unwanted movement.

4. Pin a piece of yarn with the ends at equal distances from the top of the backboard to use as a guideline for placing letters. Use a kneaded eraser to clean up drawn guidelines. (They will not leave smears.)

5. Take time to cut out pictures and graphs evenly. Ragged edges will draw attention.

6. For a framed look, use construction paper or colored paper to mat the pictures and graphs.

7. Use a decorative border of some kind, either handmade or purchased.

8. Rubber cement is a terrific adhesive, but it must be used in a vented area. If some of the rubber cement shows on the front of the backboard, let it dry and rub it into little balls for easy cleanup.

9. Never mark on uncovered foamboard. It is possible to erase the lead marking, but this will leave an impression.

Math Fair Projects and Research Activities

Chapter Fourteen

BACKBOARD PROJECT EXAMPLES

Geometry Project Example

The following is an example of a Geometry Mathematics Project:

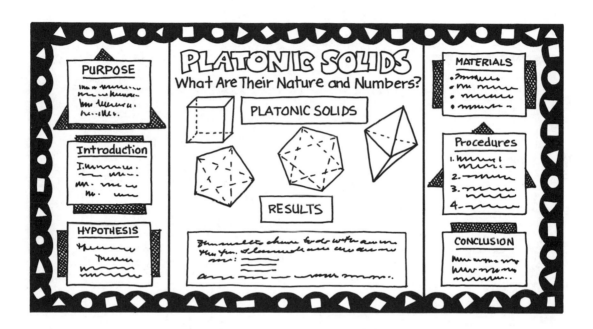

Backboard Analysis

Topic: The Platonic Solids: What Are Their Nature and Numbers?

Backboard: White

Lettering: Black for "Platonic Solids";
Red for "What Are Their Nature and Numbers?"

Border: Black Scalloped Border with Geometric Shapes

Mats: Photos, graphs, labels, and charts are matted on red construction paper.

Labels: Purpose, Introduction, Hypothesis, Platonic Solids, Results, Materials, Procedures, and Conclusion

Math Fair Projects and Research Activities

Probability Project Example

The following is an example of a Probability Mathematics Project:

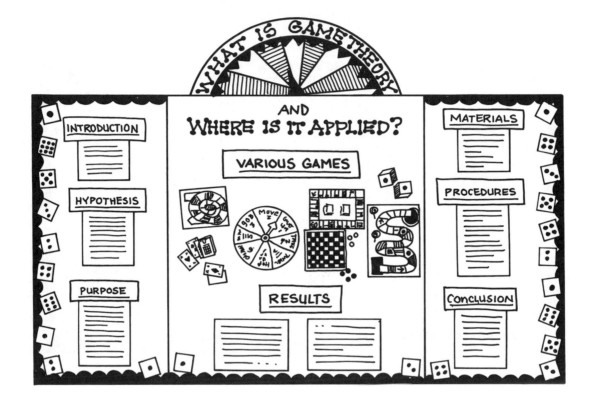

Backboard Analysis

Topic: What Is Game Theory and Where Is It Applied?

Backboard: Yellow

Lettering: Black Lettering

Border: Black Scalloped Border with Various Types of Dice

Mats: Photos, graphs, labels, and charts are matted on black construction paper.

Labels: Introduction, Hypothesis, Purpose, Various Games, Results, Materials, Procedures, and Conclusion

Number Sense Project Example

The following is an example of a Number Sense Mathematics Project:

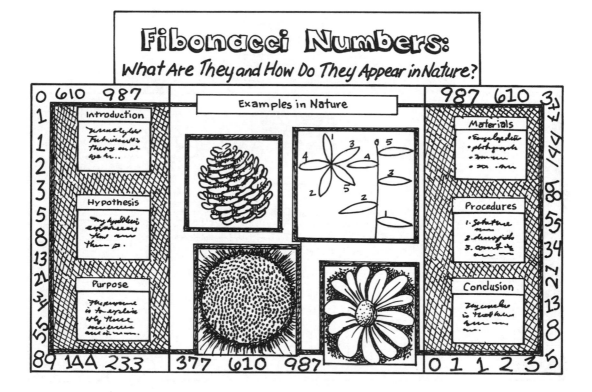

Backboard Analysis

Topic: Fibonacci Numbers: What Are They and How Do They Appear in Nature?

Backboard: White

Lettering: Blue Lettering

Border: Blue border with orange numbers

Mats: Photos, graphs, labels, and charts are matted on orange construction paper.

Labels: Introduction, Hypothesis, Purpose, Examples in Nature, Materials, Procedures, and Conclusion

Math Fair Projects and Research Activities

General Topic Project Example

The following is an example of a General Topic Mathematics Project:

Backboard Analysis

Topic: Invest In A Winner

Backboard: Black

Lettering: Green Lettering

Border: Green border with coins and bills

Mats: Graphs, charts, and labels are matted on white construction paper.

Labels: Introduction, Hypothesis, Purpose, Graphs and Charts, Interviews, Materials, Procedures, and Conclusion

Numeracy Project Example

The following is an example of a Numeracy Mathematics Project:

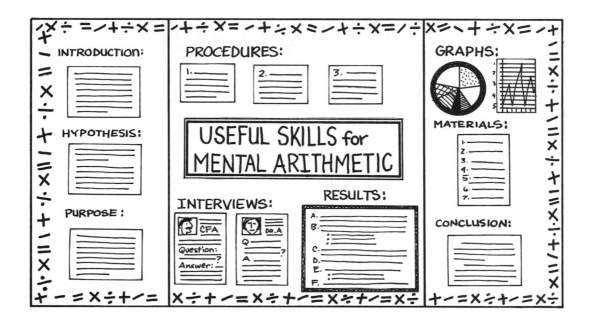

Backboard Analysis

Topic:	Useful Skills for Mental Arithmetic
Backboard:	Red
Lettering:	Blue Lettering
Border:	Mathematical Symbols border (+, −, =, x, ÷)
Mats:	Graphs, photos, and labels are matted on white construction paper.
Labels:	Introduction, Hypothesis, Purpose, Graphs, Interviews, Results, Materials, Procedures, and Conclusion

Math Fair Projects and Research Activities

APPENDIX

Sample Letter to Parents

Date: _____

Dear Parent/Guardian:

_____(Name of school)

Mathematics Fair preparations are now underway. Today your child received information about the Mathematics Fair describing the requirements, due dates, and format for the project. Participation in the Math Fair is optional; however, all students are encouraged to complete a project. A research paper and supporting documentation is required. To compete in the Mathematics Fair, a backboard is required.

Please review this information with your child as soon as possible. Your child's teacher will discuss the Mathematics Fair requirements in class. Please support and guide your child in selecting a topic and locating the needed materials. Remember: in order for your child to have a successful project, it must represent his/her work, not that of a parent or mathematics expert.

A calendar is attached which includes the due dates for each aspect of the project (choosing a topic, note taking, an outline, an abstract, a research paper, and a bibliography). May we suggest a pocket folder for use in organizing all information and research? Note cards are suggested for taking notes. Your child may need your help with proofreading his/her research paper for spelling and grammatical errors.

The Mathematics Fair is a valuable learning experience. Your cooperation and support are appreciated. When you and your child have reviewed all the information, please sign and return the bottom portion. Thank you.

Sincerely,

Dear _____ ,

I have reviewed the Math Fair information with my child,

_____ (child's name).

_____   _____
Date   Parent/Guardian Signature

Math Fair Projects and Research Activities

Tips For Parents/Guardians

1. Review all information regarding the Mathematics Fair rules with your child.

2. Assist your child in choosing a suitable topic for his/her age.

3. Allow your child time for thinking, exploring, and preparing his/her project.

4. Give encouragement, support, and guidance.

5. Realize that the goal of the Mathematics Fair Project is to help your child use and strengthen the skills he/she has learned and to develop higher-level skills. Remember: Winning a blue ribbon is not the main goal.

6. Help your child by doing the following:

    • If necessary, driving him/her to the library.

    • Helping to arrange interviews.

    • Locating Internet sites.

    • Proofreading and revising letters requesting information and/or materials.

    • Helping your child design a project that is safe and properly supervised.

    • Gathering printed materials related to his/her project.

    > **Remember:** _Assist_ your child in the completion of his or her math project. The operative word is _assist_. If the mathematics project is to be a true learning experience for your child, it is imperative that the work be completed _by the child_.

7. Proofread all material for grammatical correctness and content.

8. Be aware that your child may need assistance in delivering the project to and from school.

9. Help at your local school's Mathematics Fair. Contact your child's teacher to volunteer.

10. Encourage your child to meet all deadlines that are set by the mathematics teacher. Use a calendar to mark important dates.

11. Stress to your student the value of thanking all individuals who have given any assistance or guidance in their research and backboard production.

12. Do not worry or become upset if your child does not win a prize. Feel a sense of pride and accomplishment when the Mathematics Fair is over. Your child has earned it!

Math Fair Projects and Research Activities

Sample Letter to Student

Date: _____

Dear Student:

The information concerning the requirements, due dates, and format of the _____ (name of school) Mathematics Fair are being distributed and discussed today. Participation in the Mathematics Fair includes completing experimentation, writing a research paper, and creating a backboard.

Review the information in this packet with your parent/guardian. You may need their help and support with your topic choice and location of information. Be sure to give your parent/guardian advance notice when you need to be driven somewhere. The most successful project is one that is completed by you, and not a parent or expert. You will need note cards for taking notes and a pocket folder in which to keep your materials.

One of the goals of this project is to help you develop skills to assist you in achieving academic success. Another goal is to help you become more organized. In order to achieve these goals, you will need to do the following: create an outline; compile notes; complete research; write a well-planned paper; document and give credit to all sources; and create a visual display. When doing your research, make sure to use a variety of resources, including, but not limited to, encyclopedias, the Internet, books, and pamphlets. Be sure to ask a parent, guardian, or another adult to proofread your rough draft, as well as the final paper.

Be sure to choose a topic that interests you. Plan your assignments so that all deadlines are met. If you approach this project positively and enthusiastically, you should learn a great deal and have fun in the process.

Sincerely,

Math Fair Projects and Research Activities

Decision Making:
Topic for Research Project

1. Listed below are some choices for my Mathematics Fair Project:

   _____

   _____

   _____

2. Ask the following questions for assistance in making a decision, using the choices above. Develop a code to weigh the answers for each question. (For example: Yes, No, or Maybe). Use these answers to decide which topic to choose.

   A. Is this a topic that really interests me?

   B. What are three different sources where I might find information on this topic?

   C. Under which of the Mathematics Fair categories does this topic belong?

   D. What question can I make from this topic?

   E. Will I be able to test this topic using the scientific method?

3. My Mathematics Fair Project topic is _____

   _____

4. The reasons I have chosen this topic are as follows (refer to the questions in #2):

   A. _____

   B. _____

   C. _____

   D. _____

Student Signature _____ Date _____

Parent Signature _____ Date _____

Math Fair Projects and Research Activities

Research Proposal Sheet

Student's Name: _____ Teacher: _____

SECTION I:

Question: _____

_____

Mathematics Category: _____

Hypothesis: _____

_____

Teacher Suggestions: _____

_____

SECTION II:

Rewritten question: _____

_____

Mathematics Category: _____

Hypothesis: _____

_____

SECTION III:

List below three different resources you plan to use for your research.

1. _____

2. _____

3. _____

Teacher Suggestions: _____

_____

_____

Parent Signature _____ Date _____

Math Fair Projects and Research Activities

Mathematics Fair
RESEARCH PAPER RUBRIC
For Teachers

Teacher Name _____

Student Name _____

Category	4	3	2	1
Quality of Information	Information clearly relates to the main topic. It includes several supporting details and/or examples.	Information clearly relates to the main topic. It provides 1–2 supporting details and/or examples.	Information clearly relates to the main topic. No details and/or examples are given.	Information has little or nothing to do with the main topic.
Sources	All sources (information and graphics) are accurately documented in the desired format.	All sources (information and graphics) are accurately documented, but a few are not in the desired format.	All sources (information and graphics) are accurately documented, but many are not in the desired format.	Some sources are not accurately documented.
Mechanics	No grammatical, spelling, or punctuation errors.	Almost no grammatical, spelling, or punctuation errors	A few grammatical, spelling, or punctuation errors.	Many grammatical, spelling, or punctuation errors.

Mathematics Fair
RESEARCH PAPER RUBRIC
For Teachers

Teacher Name _____

Student Name _____

Category	4	3	2	1
Notes	Notes are recorded and organized in an extremely neat and orderly fashion.	Notes are recorded legibly and are somewhat organized.	Notes are recorded.	Notes are recorded only with peer/teacher assistance and reminders.
Internet Use	Successfully uses suggested Internet links to find information and navigates within these sites easily without assistance.	Usually able to use suggested Internet links to find information and navigates within these sites easily without assistance.	Occasionally able to use suggested Internet links to find information and navigates within these sites easily without assistance.	Needs assistance or supervision to use suggested Internet links and/or to navigate within these sites.
First Draft	Detailed draft is neatly presented and includes all required information.	Draft includes all required information and is legible.	Draft includes most required information and is legible.	Draft is missing required information and is difficult to read.

111

Math Fair Projects and Research Activities

Mathematics Fair
PROJECT RUBRIC
For Teachers

Teacher Name _____

Student Name _____

Category	4	3	2	1
Idea	Independently identified a question which was interesting to the student and which could be investigated.	Identified, with adult help, a question which was interesting to the student and which could be investigated.	Identified, with adult help, a question which could be investigated.	Identified a question that could not be tested/ investigated or one that did not merit investigation.
Description of Procedure	Procedures were outlined in a step-by-step fashion that could be followed by anyone without additional explanations. No adult help was needed to accomplish this.	Procedures were outlined in a step-by-step fashion that could be followed by anyone without additional explanations. Some adult help was needed to accomplish this.	Procedures were outlined in a step-by-step fashion, but had 1 or 2 gaps that require explanation, even after adult feedback had been given.	Procedures that were outlined were seriously incomplete or not sequential, even after adult feedback had been given.

Mathematics Fair PROJECT RUBRIC For Teachers

Teacher Name _____

Student Name _____

Category	4	3	2	1
Hypothesis Development	Independently developed a hypothesis well-substantiated by a literature review and observation of similar phenomena.	Independently developed a hypothesis somewhat substantiated by a literature review and observation of similar phenomena.	Independently developed a hypothesis somewhat substantiated by a literature review or observation of similar phenomena.	Needed adult assistance to develop a hypothesis or to do a basic literature review.
Display	Each element in the display had a function and clearly served to illustrate some aspect of the experiment. All items, graphs, etc., were neatly and correctly labeled.	Each element had a function and clearly served to illustrate some aspect of the experiment. Most items, graphs, etc., were neatly and correctly labeled.	Each element had a function and clearly served to illustrate some aspect of the experiment. Most items, graphs, etc., were correctly labeled	The display seemed incomplete or chaotic with no clear plan. Many labels were missing or incorrect.
Conclusion/ Summary	Student provided a detailed conclusion clearly based on the data and related to previous research findings and the hypothesis statement(s).	Student provided a somewhat detailed conclusion clearly based on the data and related to the hypothesis statement(s).	Student provided a conclusion with some reference to the data and the hypothesis statement(s).	No conclusion was apparent OR important details were overlooked.

Math Fair Projects and Research Activities

Suggested Roles of Responsibility

The successful completion of the Mathematics Fair project requires much support and assistance. It is strongly advised that all faculty and staff members provide as much support as possible to teachers and students. Listed below are some recommendations for involvement of staff members.

Principal and Administrators:

- Select the date for the local Mathematics Fair.
- Appoint a committee to plan and coordinate the local Mathematics Fair.
- Provide certificates for all participants in the Mathematics Fair.

Faculty and Staff:

- Help students select Mathematics Fair topics.
- Provide clear communication (in writing) to students and parents.
- Assist in cutting out letters.
- Help students obtain research materials.
- Check the first draft of the research paper and make suggestions for revisions.
- Proofread the final research paper.
- Help with the backboard design.
- Provide encouragement and praise.

Media Specialist:

- Assist students in identifying appropriate resources.
- Serve as a resource teacher for the research paper.
- Work with teachers to schedule time in the media center.

Computer Specialist:

- Assist students in the proper use of computer equipment.
- Help students with appropriate word processing software.
- Supervise student use of the Internet while in the computer lab.

Custodians:

- Help with the setup of areas that will be used for project viewing by parents, faculty, staff, and students.

Metric System for Reference:
Conversion Chart

Metric to English
Approximate Conversions from Metric Measures

Symbol	When You Know	Multiply By	To Find	Symbol
Length				
mm	millimeters	0.04	inches	in.
cm	centimeters	0.4	inches	in.
m	meters	3.3	feet	ft.
m	meters	1.1	yards	yd.
km	kilometers	0.6	miles	mi.
Area				
cm^2	square centimeters	0.16	square inches	$in.^2$
m^2	square meters	1.2	square yards	$yd.^2$
km^2	square kilometers	0.4	square miles	$mi.^2$
ha	hectares (10,000 m^2)	2.5	acres	a
Mass/Weight				
g	grams	0.03	ounces	oz.
kg	kilograms	2.2	pounds	lb.
t	tonnes (1,000 kg)	1.1	tons	T
Volume				
ml	milliliters	0.03	fluid ounces	fl. oz.
l	liters	2.1	pints	pt.
l	liters	1.06	quarts	qt.
l	liters	0.26	gallons	gal.
m^3	cubic meters	35	cubic feet	$ft.^3$
m^3	cubic meters	1.3	cubic yards	$yd.^3$
Temperature (Exact)				
°C	Celsius	$9/5$ (then add 32)	Fahrenheit	°F

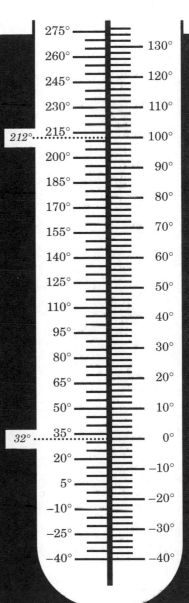

115

Math Fair Project
Recommended Websites

Mega-Mathematics

http://www.c3.lanl.gov/mega-math

Bringing "unusual and important mathematical ideas to elementary school classrooms," this site presents math in a creative and understandable way. Particularly interesting is the Open Problems section that discusses problems still not solved by mathematicians in a way all students can understand.

Bar Graph Creator

http://www.ash.udel.edu/ash/challenge/challengeframe.html

Enter data and create a bar graph with help from this site. This tutorial provides step-by-step instruction on how to create a line graph or a bar graph. If you have a Macintosh, it will even speak to you.

Math Forum: Chameleon Graphing: Coordinate Plane

http://mathforum.org/cgraph/cplane/

Dive into this introduction to graphing in the coordinate plane and meet a chameleon named Sam. Sam will help guide you through graphing points on a line, using negative numbers, and graphing points in the coordinate plane.

MathWorld

http://www.mathworld.wolfram.com

MathWorld is a comprehensive and interactive mathematics encyclopedia intended for students, educators, math enthusiasts, and researchers. Like the vibrant and constantly evolving discipline of mathematics, this site is continuously updated to include new material and incorporate new discoveries.

Making Mathematics: Mentored Research Projects

http://www2.edc.org/makingmath/default.asp

After pairing professional mathematicians with groups of students, wonderful activities emerged. Check out the projects on this site and use them in your own classroom.

Math Fair Project
Recommended Websites

21st Century Problem Solving

http://www2.hawaii.edu/suremath/home.html

This site is dedicated to helping students learn how to solve word problems.
It includes valuable teacher materials in the area of math, physics, and chemistry.

American Mathematical Society—eMath

http://e-math.ams.org

The online home of the American Mathematical Society, this site offers
information about the society, links to useful math-related places on the Web,
and organization information.

Fun With Numbers

http://www.newdream.net/~sage/old/numbers

A good source in its own way, this site features many things that you would not
want to figure out on your own, including the first 28,915 odd primes, the first 999
factorials, and 1.2 million digits of pi.

Interactive Mathematics Online

http://library.thinkquest.org/2647/

This is a very detailed and informative site that presents information on algebra,
chaos, geometry, and trigonometry. There is also a section that lets you create your
own Stereograms and some useful Java applets.

Math Archives—Topics in Mathematics

http://archives.math.utk.edu

Here is THE math resource site on the Web. It has hundreds of links (fully searchable)
in forty different categories ranging from Algebra to Partial Differential Equations.

NetTrekker—A Search Engine for Students and Teachers

http://www.nettrekker.com

This is a powerful search engine for both teachers and students. Elementary, middle,
and high school math topics are included. A nominal subscription fee is required.

Math Fair Projects and Research Activities

Math Fair Student Checklist

Date: _____

Teacher Name: _____

Student Name: _____

Project Title: _____

CATEGORY	RESPONSIBILITIES

Appearance
- ☐ Text areas and graphic areas are balanced.
- ☐ The words on the backboard are easy to read.
- ☐ The words on the backboard are spelled correctly.
- ☐ The background does not compete with the text or graphics.
- ☐ Titles and headings are easy to distinguish from other text.
- ☐ There is enough time to read and see everything on the backboard.

Organization
- ☐ I made an outline to organize my thoughts and ideas.
- ☐ My presentation was a clear explanation of the topic.
- ☐ My presentation had a clear answer to a research question.
- ☐ My organization was easy for others to follow.
- ☐ I used a bibliography.

Resources
- ☐ I used a variety of resources.
- ☐ I used resources that showed different perspectives.
- ☐ I used resources that were reliable and credible.
- ☐ I used up-to-date resources.
- ☐ I used electronic resources (Internet, CD-ROM).
- ☐ I used print resources (textbooks, books, magazines, newspapers).
- ☐ I used documentaries or news interviews.
- ☐ I used materials in accordance with copyright.
- ☐ I cited my resources.

Math Fair Projects and Research Activities

Judge's Score Sheet

Student Name: _____ Teacher: _____

Project Title: _____

		Above Average—Average			Fair—Needs Improvement		
Scientific Thought	• Complete understanding of the problem, mathematical ideas, and processes is shown.	6	5	4	3	2	1
	• Measurements/observations are accurate.	6	5	4	3	2	1
	• Goals and objectives are well defined.	6	5	4	3	2	1
	• Conclusions are accurately based on data.	6	5	4	3	2	1
Effectiveness	• Explanation of project is clear and concise.	6	5	4	3	2	1
	• The nature of the problem, how the problem is solved, and the conclusion are clearly communicated.	6	5	4	3	2	1
	• There is evidence that data was collected from several sources.	6	5	4	3	2	1
	• The project follows the scientific method.	6	5	4	3	2	1
Creativity	• The project topic is unique or original.	6	5	4	3	2	1
	• The approach to answering the question is creative.	6	5	4	3	2	1
	• Originality is shown in the design of the project.	6	5	4	3	2	1
	• The student goes beyond the requirements of the problem.	6	5	4	3	2	1
Clarity	• Problem, procedures, data, and conclusion are presented clearly and in a logical order.	6	5	4	3	2	1
	• Project visually shows an analysis of the data in tables, charts, or pictures with clear headings.	6	5	4	3	2	1
	• Backboard is neat and attractive.	6	5	4	3	2	1
	• Research paper shows evidence of research, experimentation, and analysis.	6	5	4	3	2	1
	Overall Score for Mathematics Project ➞	6	5	4	3	2	1

Math Fair Projects and Research Activities

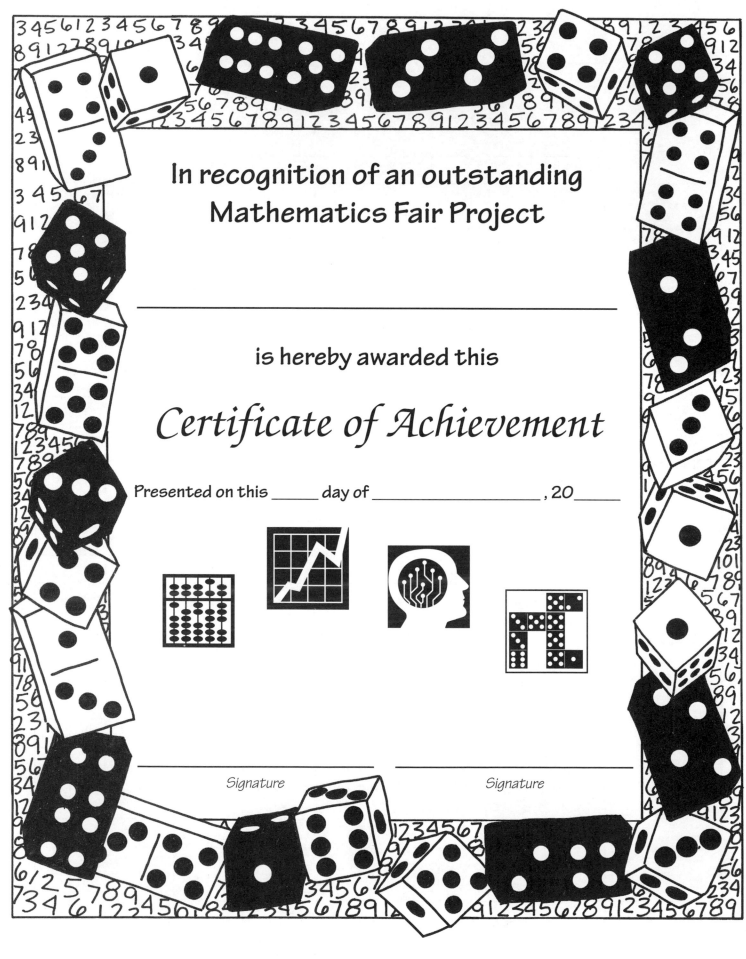

In recognition of an outstanding
Mathematics Fair Project

_____

is hereby awarded this

Certificate of Achievement

Presented on this _____ day of _____ , 20 _____

_____   _____
Signature   *Signature*

Answer Key

Can You Write a Good Topic Question?

A good mathematics topic is one which enables you to use everyday experiences to compare, investigate, or model the question. Read the real-world situations below and write a possible topic question.

1. Lee Nakato goes to a Japanese school where he studies mathematics using the Kumon Method. Lennie Mitchell, his neighbor and best friend, goes to the middle school down the street and studies mathematics the "traditional" way.

Topic Question: *How does the Kumon Method of mathematics compare to the "traditional" method of mathematics?*

2. In August, compare the mean, median, and range of heights for males and females in your class at school. Measure again in January.

Topic Question: *How do the heights of male and female students compare in mean, median, and range over 6 months?*

3. The game "Rock, Paper, Scissors" has three moves. Use statistics to show how many times "scissors" comes up.

Topic Question: *Can the game "Rock, Paper, Scissors" be used to demonstrate statistics?*

PAGE 16

---

4. In an experiment, Andy flips a coin 10 times and gets "heads" 7 times. He knows that the hypothetical odds should be 5 "heads" in 10 flips.

Topic Question: *Is the probability of "heads" really 50–50 in a coin toss?*

5. Kimberly reaches into a bag of colored candies and gets a red one. The next time she also gets a red one.

Topic Question: *What is the probability of reaching into a bag of colored candies and selecting a particular color?*

PAGE 17

Mathematicians Through the Ages
How Good Are Your Research Skills?

Directions: Use an encyclopedia or the Internet to match these famous mathematicians with their major accomplishments.

e 1. Baron Gottfried Wilhelm Von Leibniz

b 2. Jean Victor Poncelet

g 3. Aristotle

c 4. Pythagoras

f 5. Pierre Simon de Laplace

h 6. George Boole

j 7. John Napier

a 8. Karl Weierstrass

d 9. Ptolemy

i 10. Charles Babbage

a. His mathematics work influenced the production of atomic energy. (1815–1897)

b. He is best remembered for his theory on the continuity of numbers. (1788–1867)

c. He is best know for his geometric theorem of a right triangle. (588–507 B.C.)

d. He was the first to give pi an estimated value of 3.1416. (100–146)

e. He is credited with inventing Calculus, the chief advancement in mathematics during the first half of the 18th Century. (1646–1716)

f. A French mathematician who, with Bernoulli, was one of the originators of the field of probability. (1749–1867)

g. A great Greek philosopher who laid the foundation for most of the branches of science and philosophy known today. (384–322 B.C.)

h. An English mathematician who helped develop modern symbolic logic. (1815–1865)

i. He invented a calculating machine that was the forerunner of today's computers. (1792–1871)

j. He invented a multiplication device for improving the Abacus which was the forerunner of the slide rule. (1550–1617)

PAGE 26

Mathematicians Through the Ages
Timeline of Mathematicians

Directions: Place the mathematicians listed below on the timeline showing when they were born.

Democritus — Aristotle — Euclid — Ptolemy

500 B.C.   400 B.C.   300 B.C.   200 B.C.   100 B.C.   0 A.D.   100 A.D.

Boethius   Baskara

200 A.D.   300 A.D.   400 A.D.   500 A.D.   600 A.D.   700 A.D.   800 A.D.

Leonardo of Pisa — Roger Bacon — Nicole Oresme — Nicholas Copernicus — Galileo Galilei

900 A.D.   1000 A.D.   1100 A.D.   1200 A.D.   1300 A.D.   1400 A.D.   1500 A.D.

William Jones — Karl Gauss — Charles Babbage — George Boole — Albert Einstein — Vannevar Bush

1600 A.D.   1700 A.D.   1800 A.D.   1900 A.D.   2000 A.D.   2100 A.D.   2200 A.D.

Aristotle 384 B.C.	Albert Einstein 1879 A.D.
Charles Babbage 1792 A.D.	Euclid 300 B.C.
Roger Bacon 1214 A.D.	Galileo Galilei 1564 A.D.
Boethius Bhaskara 475 A.D.	Karl Friedrich Gauss 1777 A.D.
George Boole 1815 A.D.	William Jones 1675 A.D.
Nicholas Copernicus 1473 A.D.	Leonardo of Pisa 1175 A.D.
Democritus 460 B.C.	Nicole Oresme 1323 A.D.
Vannevar Bush 1890 A.D.	Ptolemy 100 A.D.

PAGE 27

Math Fair Projects and Research Activities

Answer Key

Famous Women Mathematicians

Directions: Choose a famous woman mathematician from the alphabetical list on the previous pages. Research the contributions she made to mathematics. Record your facts on the graphic organizer below.

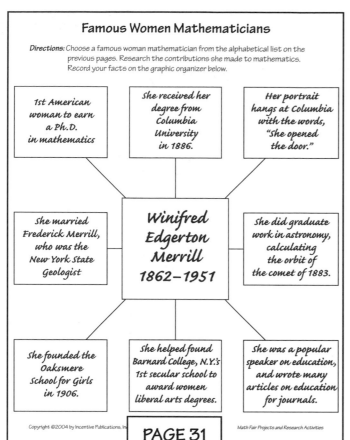

1st American woman to earn a Ph.D. in mathematics

She received her degree from Columbia University in 1886.

Her portrait hangs at Columbia with the words, "She opened the door."

She married Frederick Merrill, who was the New York State Geologist

Winifred Edgerton Merrill 1862–1951

She did graduate work in astronomy, calculating the orbit of the comet of 1883.

She founded the Oaksmere School for Girls in 1906.

She helped found Barnard College, N.Y.'s 1st secular school to award women liberal arts degrees.

She was a popular speaker on education, and wrote many articles on education for journals.

Math Fair Projects and Research Activities

PAGE 31

Note-Taking Practice

Use your judgment in choosing the most important and least important statements. Read the article carefully, then answer the questions that follow.

Probability Theory

Most of the early important work in probability theory was done by Fermat (1601–1665) and another French mathematician, Blaise Pascal (1623–1662). Some work had been done in this area before by the gambler-mathematician Girolamo Cardano (1501–1576), an Italian.

A gambler would have good reason to be interested in probability theory. This branch of mathematics is concerned with chance. It finds out what the chances are of one result happening out of a number of possible results. When a gambler uses dice or cards, he is interested in chance. For example, he may want to know his chances for rolling a 7 instead of a 10 with a pair of dice.

Probability theory is used not only to find betting odds, but also in daily weather reports to give the likelihood of rain. It is used in many other areas, such as science and business.

Therefore, one could say that probability deals with chances. For example, if you have 5 possible solutions to a situation, then the chance that one of them will happen is 1 out of 5. When using probability, the symbol for this is $\frac{1}{5}$. This symbol is a fraction and should be used like any fraction.

What if you were to toss a coin? Obviously there are two possible results. The coin can land tails up or heads up. The probability that the coin will land tails up is 1 out of 2 or $\frac{1}{2}$. The probability that it will land heads up is also $\frac{1}{2}$.

1. What is the probability of a coin landing tails up?
   The probability of a coin landing tails up is 1 out of 2, or $\frac{1}{2}$.

2. Who did the earlier important work in probability theory?
   Fermat and Blaise Pascal did the early work in probability.

3. Name two of the three ways mentioned that probability can be used today.
   Probability is used in business and science.

4. Why would a gambler be interested in the probability theory?
   A gambler may want to know his chances for rolling a certain number with dice.

Math Fair Projects and Research Activities

PAGE 47

Note-Taking Practice

When taking notes, begin by skimming the material in order to get a general idea of the content. When reading the material for the second time, read more carefully in order to find the main points and details. Instead of writing complete sentences, make brief notes.

On the right side of this page, take notes on the article below. Remember to use brief notes instead of complete sentences. Check the article for main ideas, cue words, and punctuation. Remember to use quotation marks for direct quotes.

Leonard Fibonacci	Notes
Leonard Fibonacci, who is responsible for introducing an essential tool for mathematical progress, lived in Pisa, Italy. He made a major contribution to the development of modern mathematics. Not much is known about his life except what he wrote in his best-known work, *Book of Calculations*. The publication of this book was a landmark in both the history of mathematics and the history of the Middle Ages.	*Leonard Fibonacci* *Pisa, Italy* *made contribution to develop modern math* *wrote book — Book of Calculations a milestone in math and in Middle Ages*
Fibonacci traveled around the Mediterranean Sea. He visited many places including Egypt, Syria, Sicily, and Constantinople. Everywhere he went he talked about mathematics. When he returned home, Leonard began to write about the new information he had learned. The purpose of his book was to introduce and explain the Hindu-Arabic numbers. Fibonacci included numerous examples of how Roman numerals could be translated into these new numbers. He also explained various operations that could be completed with these numbers.	*traveled — Mediterranean Sea* *learned more about math* *brought back information on Hindu-Arabic numbers* *book included: explanations examples operations*
Fibonacci's most important achievement in number theory was what is known as a type of algebra called Diophantine analysis. This type of algebra deals with indeterminates, equations in two or more unknowns that require a solution using whole numbers or common fractions.	*important information on Diophantine analysis*

PAGE 48

Outlining Practice

After reading the information about the history of algebra, complete the following outline.

I. Egyptian Algebra
   A. *Rhind Papyrus*
      1. *Linear equation*
      2. *Rhetorical*
      3. *Verbal solutions*
   B. *Cairo Papyrus*

II. Babylonian Algebra
   A. More Advanced
      1. *Quadratic formula*
      2. *Higher degree equations*
   B. Like Egyptians
      1. *Rhetorical*
      2. *Positive rational numbers*

III. Greek Algebra
   A. *Irrational numbers*
   B. *Quadratic equations*
   C. *Deductive reasoning*

IV. Diophantine Algebra
   A. *Syncopated style*
   B. Arithmetica
      1. *Indeterminate equations*
      2. *Different solutions*

V. Hindu Algebra
   A. *Base ten*
   B. *Zero*
   C. Negative Numbers
   D. *Irrational numbers*
   E. *Symbols*
   F. Quadratic Equations
      1. *Two roots*
      2. *Indeterminate*

PAGE 52

Answer Key

Outlining Practice

To further test your knowledge of outlines, parts of two outlines are given below. The outlines are in scrambled order. For the first outline (on the left), the form is supplied. For the second outline, create the form from scratch.

Importance	*Suggestion: Place the Roman numerals first for each of the three main topics. Leave spaces for the subtopics under each main topic.*
Assumptions	
Perpendicular Lines	
Basic Elements	
Quadrilaterals	

Measuring Size and Space	Tools
Systems	Length and Distance
Volume	Derived Measurements
Basic Measurements	Area
Making Measurements	Using Other Measurements

Definitions
Angle Bisection
Theorems
Triangles
Constructions

Geometry

I. _Importance_

II. Geometric Proof
   A. _Basic Elements_
   B. _Definitions_
   C. _Assumptions_
   D. _Theorems_

III. _Constructions_
   A. _Angle Bisections_
   B. Line Bisection
   C. _Perpendicular line_

IV. Geometric Figures
   A. _Quadrangles_
   B. _Triangles_

Measurements

I. *Making Measurements*
   A. *Systems*
   B. *Tools*

II. *Measuring Size and Space*
   A. *Length and Distance*
   B. *Area*
   C. *Volume*

III. *Using Other Measurements*
   A. *Basic Measurements*
   B. *Derived Measurements*

Math Fair Projects and Research Activities

PAGE 53

Introductory Paragraph Practice

While writing the introductory paragraph, please keep in mind that the introduction should include background information and the reasons for the choice of study. Conclude by stating the hypothesis.

Directions: Edit the first draft paragraph. While rewriting the paragraph, feel free to change any of the words, place the sentences in a more logical order, and remove any sentences that do not agree with the main topic. Also correct any errors in spelling, capitalization, and punctuation.

His research, centered around things that would affect the timing of a pendulum's swing. Pendullums are used in time measurment as well as musical measurement. In the past, they have been used to detect earthquakers and also to measure the strength of gravity. Galileo galilei became fascinated with pendulums and researched its behavior. Galileo was forced to leave the University of Pisa in 1585! From Galileo's research he found that the only thing that would change a pendulum's behavior was a change in the length of the string. Were Galileo's Experiments accurate and how are pendulums still used in today's society?

Pendulums are used in time measurement as well as musical measurement. In the past, they have been used to detect earthquakes and also to measure the strength of gravity. Galileo Galilei became fascinated with pendulums and researched their behavior. His research was centered around investigating anything that would affect the timing of a pendulum's swing. From his research, Galileo found that the only thing that would change a pendulum's behavior was a change in the length of the string. Were Galileo's experiments accurate? How are pendulums still used in today's society?

PAGE 58

Conclusion Practice

Remember that the concluding paragraph should briefly summarize results. It should include discussion of whether or not the data supported the hypothesis. Finally, include what the next steps in experimentation may be.

Directions: Read the following conclusion. Feel free to change any of the words, place the sentences in a more logical order, and remove any sentences that do not agree with the main topic. Also, correct any errors in spelling, capitalization, and punctuation.

It is amazing that one simple number can shape our world, It is the length between the mathamatical world and the human perciption of perfection. The Golden Ratio continues to open doors in our understanding of life and the universe. The thorax and the abdomen in most bees is nearly equal to the golden ratio. For the last several thousand years, the Golden Ratio has captured the interest and wonder of humankind and it still has not lost its touch. people every day are still seeking for the treasures that are yet found in the Golden Ratio? When think we have discovered and understand all the little hidden secrets of the Divine Proportion, it turns up and surprises us in a unexpected places

It is amazing that one simple number can shape our world so thoroughly. It is the link between the mathematical world and the human perception of perfection. The Golden Ratio continues to open doors in our understanding of life and the universe. When we think we have discovered and understand all the little hidden secrets of the Divine Proportion, it turns up and surprises us in unexpected places. For the last several thousand years, the Golden Ratio has captured the interest and wonder of humankind and it still has not lost its touch. People every day are still seeking the treasures that are yet to be found in the Golden Ratio.

Math Fair Projects and Research Activities

PAGE 59

Abstract Practice

When writing your abstract, remember that an abstract is a concise summary of the entire research project. It should include the following: purpose, hypothesis, procedure, data, conclusions, and possible applications.

Directions: Edit the following abstract. While rewriting the abstract, feel free to change any of the words, place the sentences in a more logical order, and remove any sentences that do not agree with the main topic. Also, correct any errors in spelling, capitalization, and punctuation.

We recorded the time needed for the vertical descent of the Arrow during each shot or drop. The purpose of this experiment was to study the behavior of a Nerf-gun arrow under two different conditions: dropped and fired horizontally! Our team attempted to prove that the two arrows will use the same amount of time to descend to the ground. After several trials. the team recorded their experimentation of several varying heights of fireing and droping our arrows. Shooting Nerf-guns is fun! After graphical and experimental comparisons of the data, we found the arrow to indicate the results we expected. analyzing the data indicated that horizontal velocity acted upon the arrow separate from gravitational pull.

The purpose of this experiment was to study the behavior of a Nerf-gun arrow under two different conditions: dropped and fired horizontally. Our team attempted to prove that the two arrows would use the same amount of time to descend to the ground. After several trials, the team recorded the results of our experimentation of firing and dropping arrows from several varying heights. We recorded the time needed for the vertical descent of the arrow during each shot or drop. After graphical and experimental comparisons of the data, we found that the results were as we expected. Analysis of the data indicated that horizontal velocity acted upon the arrow separately from gravitational pull.

PAGE 60

Math Fair Projects and Research Activities

Answer Key

Writing Bibliographical Entries

When writing a research paper, it is necessary to include a bibliography at the end. The bibliography is a list of all the sources used when gathering information for the paper. Bibliographies follow a special format and list important information about the sources. Write bibliographical entries for the sources listed below. As a guide, refer to pages 65–66.

1. A book called Addition and Subtraction was written by Abbey Cuss and published by Model Publishing Company, of Countville, in 1999.

   Cuss, Abbey. Addition and Subtraction.

   Countville: Model publishing Company, 1999.

2. "Using Pi" written by Di Ameter was found Online and published by Area Publishers in Circle City, on May 13, 2001.

   Ameter, Di. "Using Pi." Online. Area Publishers.

   13 May 2001.

3. A pamphlet entitled Using Equations by Lyn E. Er was produced by The Vari Able Publishing Corporation in Algebratown in 2003.

   Er, Lyn E. Using Equations. Algebratown:

   The Vari Able Publishing Corporation, 2003.

4. Appearing in Vol. 15 of Theorem Encyclopedia in 1999 was an article on "The Pythagorean Theorem" written by Hypot E. Nuse and found on pages 201–211.

   Nuse, Hypot E. "The Pythagorean Theorem."

   Theorem Encyclopedia. 1999.

5. Published by Mandelbrot Sets Publishing of Koch Curve City, Snow Flake wrote an article entitled "Drawing Fractals" for Simple Equations Magazine in December of 1999.

   Flake, Snow. "Drawing Fractals." Simple Equations

   Magazine. December, 1999.

6. Noisy Times contained an article in Section D, page 3 on "Parabolic Reflector Microphones" written by S. P. Orting Events and produced by Sound Publishers on January 21, 1995.

   Events, S. P. Orting. "Parabolic Reflector Microphones."

   Noisy Times. January 21, 1995, Sec. D, p. 3.

7. A book on Galileo Galilei was jointly written by Johannes Kepler and P. Tolemy and published by Pendulum Brothers, Pisa, Italy in 1995.

   Kepler, Johannes and P. Tolemy. Galileo Galilei.

   Pisa, Italy: Pendulum Brothers, 1995.

8. P. L. Atonic was interviewed by Archi Median at 10:00 AM on June 17, 2001 in Solids Falls, Vermont.

   Atonic, P. L. Solid Falls, Vermont. June 17, 2001.

9. I received an email through Mathmet, entitled "Card Tricks" on July 4, 2003. Persi Diaconis wrote it on June 30, 2003. It was then received from statisticiansgroup.comp. magic.tricks

   Diaconis, Persi. "Card Tricks." [Online] Available

   email: statisticiansgroup.comp.magic.tricks.

   June 30, 2003

Bibliography Practice

Julian really needs help writing a bibliographic list. He used the sources listed in the paragraph below while writing his math research paper: "The Golden Ratio." For the bibliography, use the lines below.

In the book Golden Ratio by Joseph Wassermann, Paul Robert Trumble, and Barbara Nelson-Klein, Julian found the information. The book was published by Wolfram Publishing Company in Hanover, in 1999. He also found an article entitled "Fibonacci Sequence" in World Book Encyclopedia produced by Childcraft International, Inc. in 1993. The third source was the book Phi: That Golden Number written by Isabelle Frances Peterson in 2002 and published by Greg & Collins Publishing of Atlanta. He found an article entitled Harrison's Golden Ratio Extravaganza on the internet at http://biology.mathforum.worldofmath/uga.edu/page3/html. Finally, Julian located an article entitled "Using Golden Ratio" in the Encyclopedia Britannica, Vol. 8, pages 112–118. It was published in 2003.

Bibliography

"Fibonacci Sequence." World Book Encyclopedia. Childcraft
International, Inc., 1993.

"Harrison's Golden Ratio Extravaganza." Internet.
http://biology.mathforum.worldofmath/uga.edu/page3/html.

Peterson, Isabelle Francis. Phi: That Golden Number.
Atlanta: Greg and Collins Pubishing, 2002.

"Using Golden Ratio." Encyclopedia Brittanica. Vol. 8,
pages 112-118.

Nelson-Klein, Barbara, Paul Robert Trumble, and
Joseph Wassermann. The Golden Ratio. Hanover:
Wolfram Publishing, 1999.

Mathematics Fair Project Title Cards

Note to the Teacher: *Reproduce these title cards on card stock and give to each student doing a mathematics project.*

INTRODUCTION

PURPOSE

HYPOTHESIS

PROBLEM

Math Fair Projects and Research Activities

INTERVIEWS

RESULTS

MATERIALS

PROCEDURES

CONCLUSION

GRAPH

CHART

Math Fair Projects and Research Activities